W9-AUI-858

Additional Praise for *The Growth Mindset*

What some top leaders are saying about Rick Capozzi:

"The way Rick Capozzi frames the disruptive technologies facing the financial industry with the core fundamentals, people skills, quality of advice, and an exceptional client experience is brilliant. Rick has frontline experience building great businesses. Practical and timely, this book deserves to be read by every financial advisor who is serious about growth."

—Matt Oechsli, CEO, Oechsli Institute

"After more than 40 years of selecting and developing leaders, I can say without reservation that Rick Capozzi has written a magnificent book on what it takes to be a leader in times of challenge and disruption. I have worked with Rick and for him over the years and I have seen first hand his ability to practice what he preaches. This book is a must read. It's a blueprint to greater success, if you absorb it, evaluate your own leadership behavior against it, and put it to work."

—Jim Carbonaro, former SVP head of Leadership Development at Morgan Stanley, Wells Fargo, and UBS

"*The Growth Mindset* is a crucial almanac. I highly recommend everyone in the wealth management and asset management industry read it. The book addresses many thought-provoking issues. For example, what was recently presented as the centerpiece of the value proposition presented to clients is rapidly moving to a commodity. Rick's years of experience and success in multiple leadership roles in this industry of change have given him license to produce this playbook to assist professionals in building and/or evolving successful business models to maximize the client experience. This is a must-read if you're serious about growth. Enjoy the journey!"

—Mark Pennington, Former MD Partner, Lord, Abbett & Co. LLC

"*The Growth Mindset* is a must-read. Rick leverages his vast experiences to outline the attributes of successful leaders. He tackles the challenges and disruption facing our industry, and offers sage counsel on how organizations should respond. Rick uses leadership quotes, interviews, and personal anecdotes to bring new concepts to life."

—Anthony B. Davidow, CIMA®, Alternative Beta & Asset Allocation strategist, Schwab Center for Financial Research

"Capozzi captures how leadership does make a difference in an ever-changing industry experiencing extraordinary pace and magnitude with the current pivots. No matter who you are, or how successful, this book will inspire you to open your mind to larger possibilities."

—Craig Pfeiffer, CEO of the Money Management Institute (MMI) and chairman of Advisors Ahead

"Rick Capozzi has written an outstanding roadmap for leaders in the wealth management industry. Capozzi has a unique talent for making the complex simple. He masterfully inspires you to stretch your capabilities and reach for greater heights. He advises business leaders to adopt a growth mindset, embrace leadership fundamentals, and create value for their clients. His guidance to focus on the specific target market and to "be *all* things to *some* people" is critical. This book should be required reading in all MBA programs where we are preparing the next generation of wealth management leaders.

—Ellen D. Durnin, Ph.D., dean of the Business School,
Southern Connecticut State University.

"Whether you are an experienced advisor, leader, or just starting out in the business, Rick has produced a fantastic book for all. This is by far one of the best books in sharing proven and practical strategies to grow a truly holistic and consultative business. Rick will inspire you to reexamine your business model. He shows you how to deal with fee compression and automated advice. Ultimately he will help you master the Growth Mindset, which will change your life and your clients."

—Richard G. Dragotta, ChFC, CRPC, founder INC
Advisors, principal LPL Financial

"As a result of Rick's work, today, every one of our advisors is in a much better position to compete. We've seen a tremendous improvement in ownership and accountability of our people, leading to increased client satisfaction and loyalty. Rick's book is timely and will further advance the sales and service culture of First Tennessee Bank."

—Rhomes Aur, CEO, FTB Advisors

Change is happening at an unbelievable pace, and few industries are experiencing change as much as financial services. Leaders need to be equipped to navigate this change in order to get results and help others adapt to the future. Having coached and trained thousands of leaders, advisors and staff in financial services I have had the privilege to be exposed to some of the most impressive thinkers and implementers in the industry. Rick Capozzi ranks as one of the best. His book *The Growth Mindset* has never been needed more than it is today. The challenges are big for the future and that means so are the opportunities. Leaders who study this book will be able to help themselves and others flourish in an environment where many others will flounder. In the end, if leaders find these opportunities and help others navigate them well, then the clients will be the ones who benefit the most. And that is the most noble calling of this business.

—Tim Ursiny, Ph.D., RCC, CBC, Founder, Advantage Coaching & Training, Author of multiple books including his most recent, *Soft Souls Living in a Harsh World*

The Chinese proverb says to know the road ahead, ask those coming back. Elite Financial Advisors did not become successful by accident. They all found someone with greater wisdom and greater experience to guide them to the top. Regardless of one's tenure and accomplishments, every advisor needs a mentor. I have known Rick Capozzi for many years and I consider him to be one of the best, if not the best, mentor in our industry. It doesn't matter if you are new and fighting to establish your credentials or if you are a top quintile advisor striving for greater heights, you need Rick as a mentor and the mentorship begins right here, with *The Growth Mindset*.

—Don Connelly, Former SVP of marketing at Putnam, National Speaker and Coach.

The Growth Mindset

The Growth Mindset

Leadership Makes a Difference in Wealth Management

Rick Capozzi

WILEY

Published by John Wiley & Sons, Inc., Hoboken, New Jersey.

Published simultaneously in Canada.

For general information on our other products and services or for technical support, please contact our Customer Care Department within the United States at (800) 762-2974, outside the United States at (317) 572-3993, or fax (317) 572-4002.

Wiley publishes in a variety of print and electronic formats and by print-on-demand. Some material included with standard print versions of this book may not be included in e-books or in print-on-demand. If this book refers to media such as a CD or DVD that is not included in the version you purchased, you may download this material at http://booksupport.wiley.com. For more information about Wiley products, visit www.wiley.com.

Library of Congress Cataloging-in-Publication Data is available:

Names: Capozzi, Rick, 1960– author.
Title: The growth mindset : leadership makes a difference in wealth management / Rick Capozzi.
Description: Hoboken, New Jersey : John Wiley & Sons, Inc., 2017. | Includes index. |
Identifiers: LCCN 2017023320 (print) | LCCN 2017036340 (ebook) | ISBN 9781119422013 (pdf) | ISBN 9781119421986 (epub) | ISBN 9781119421979 (cloth)
Subjects: LCSH: Financial planners. | Investment advisors. | Leadership. | Financial services industry—Management.
Classification: LCC HG179.5 (ebook) | LCC HG179.5 .C357 2017 (print) | DDC 332.6—dc23
LC record available at https://lccn.loc.gov/2017023320

Cover Design: Wiley
Cover Image: Tree icon © bubaone/iStockphoto; Ornament © mashuk/iStockphoto

Printed in the United States of America.

10 9 8 7 6 5 4 3 2 1

In memory of my mother, the most wonderful gift on earth.

To my loving family, they mean the world to me. Bianca and Emilia for the joy they bring into my life and Barbara for her unconditional support and love.

To the authentic trusted advisors who show up and make it happen.

Contents

Artwork By Bianca Capozzi

Advice from a Tree

Dear Friend
Stand Tall and Proud
Sink your roots deeply into the Earth
Reflect the light of your true nature
Think long term
Go out on a limb
Remember your place among all living beings
Embrace with joy the changing seasons
For each yields its own abundance
The Energy and Birth of Spring
The Growth and Contentment of Summer
The Wisdom to let go like leaves in the Fall
The Rest and Quiet renewal of Winter

Feel the wind and the sun
And delight in their presence
Look up at the moon that shines down upon you
And the mystery of the stars at night
Seek nourishment from the good things in life
Simple pleasures
Earth, fresh air, light
Be Content with your natural beauty
Drink plenty of water
Let your limbs sway and dance in the breezes
Be flexible
Remember your roots
Enjoy the view!

Ilan Shamir © Ilan Shamir,
www.yourtruenature.com

Introduction

"Vision doesn't usually come as a lightning bolt. Rather it comes as a slow crystallization of life challenges that we one day recognize as a beautiful diamond with great value to ourselves and others."

—*Dr. Michael Norwood*

Within the wealth management industry how we deliver advice and a superior client experience is fundamentally changing. These changes will have a profound impact on the role the advisor plays in serving the high-net-worth market. The greatest transfer of wealth in the history of the world is under way as baby boomers age and pass their assets to the next generation. This transfer of wealth combined with the rise of automated advice in the form of robo- and virtual advisors, online services offering algorithm-based portfolio management, and a host of other factors will create one

of the most significant disruptions to hit the financial services industry. In the face of this disruption, the future of
our industry demands that advisors and managers evolve,
lead, and serve. Those advisors who can deliver holistic
and customized advice beyond investment solutions will be
positioned to capitalize on change and win the lion's share
of the high-net-worth market.

I have seen a lot of change over the past three decades
but nothing like the amount of change happening right
now. This tsunami of change is already making its way to
the financial industry shoreline, and it promises to swallow
up those industry professionals unprepared to act in the face
of challenge and disruption. If you are reading *The Growth
Mindset: Leadership Makes a Difference in Wealth Management,*
it's because you want to survive the rip current and grow
your business in response to this sea change in front of us.
Of course, many people may not be ready. Leaders across
the industry are struggling with fee compression, lack of
differentiation, increased competition, technological revolution, and a sophisticated and demanding global client—all
of which makes the future of wealth management demand
that leaders and advisors evolve and master the fundamentals.
The future model will focus on delivering customized value
in which the client ultimately benefits. High-net-worth
clients are not focused on cost; they are, however, focused
on value. This book helps you differentiate yourself from the
crowd not only by delivering advice and service but also by
showing you what the clients value most.

Disruption, like a tsunami, can resemble a rapidly rising
tide—a series of waves whose impact and destructive
power can be enormous. Only the strong leaders tend to

survive this type of disruption. From a position of strength, the leader must fight against the power of the current with the appropriate response—actions and behaviors associated only with great leaders, many of whom I have been fortunate enough to observe. These types of leaders will be absolutely required for an organization or individual to achieve success.

Whatever you do, don't let yourself or your firm become a casualty to complacency. Many leaders and firms tend to hit a plateau between seven and ten years in the business. Adopt and practice the leadership principles in this book that resonate with you the most, and lead your team beyond the plateau to achieve greater success.

Industry Challenges and Disruption

A leader's greatest motivation is a new challenge and greatest liability is insecurity. Whether he or she faces the challenges of the future head-on with a healthy sense of confidence and optimism or retreats with pessimism and doubt ultimately determines success or failure. If you're a CEO or CIO of your own firm, you probably spend a significant amount of time developing strategies to not only help your firm grow but also protect your clients and employees. Some of the most relevant topics today include regulations, mobile platforms, cloud storage, artificial intelligence, blockchain technology, and cyber-security. The incredibly fast rate of change, which requires a great deal of consideration and action, does not allow us the luxury of sitting back without investing back into the business and attracting the right talent.

Over the past 34 years working in the financial services, I have witnessed the necessity to adapt to change firsthand while working with top executives at the most prominent firms. Having served nearly all facets of senior leadership in many positions all the way up to the C-suite, I am now witnessing a time unlike any I have seen before, primarily marked by the commoditization of our services by disruptive technologies. The challenges at hand are very real and have the potential to cause a changing of the guard, an army of increased competition and new players, luring our existing clients with an arsenal of choice. History is littered with examples of once-stalwart, seemingly unassailable companies that simply failed to address change effectively and ultimately disappeared. Organizations that lack the right leadership assets—leaders who cannot face the following challenges head-on—will not be able to compete effectively in:

- The war for top talent
- New technologies that promise to make current advice models obsolete
- Passive versus active money management
- Disruptive fintech organizations
- Fee compression and reduced margins
- Escalating regulatory landscape
- Sophisticated, value-minded investors
- Increased competition and difficulty being distinctive

The financial technology industry promises to deliver financial services more efficiently and more cost-effectively than the traditional investment advisory model while enhancing the client experience with better data reporting, greater transparency, and streamlined processes. We have been operating in an environment for the past 50 years that for the most part has been generous to the asset management and wealth management industry. But today we are dealing with a plethora of automated investing platforms, the shift of passive versus active management, fee and margin compression, and more regulatory change in the past five years than the past 40 years. Clients are increasingly more sophisticated and have access to virtually any information. Therefore, the future client will demand value for a reasonable fee and those that cannot deliver value will be forced to reduce the fee or look for a different profession. For example, investment management services should not be the only core value proposition going forward. That alone will continue to become increasingly more commoditized. Therefore, if that's your only value proposition, you will only be able to compete on price.

As an advisor, you have a responsibility to stay on the cutting edge of product innovation, process innovation, and service innovation. You have a direct responsibility to lead your clients and your team to model the behavior necessary to win the battle in front of you. Anyone in the organization can lead and make a difference if he or she is willing to adapt, grow, and learn what I call the *growth mindset*.

One of the most important themes of this book is that you don't become a leader by slipping on an impressive title, because we have all worked for people who are completely incompetent yet somehow occupy a prestigious position of authority. Leadership cannot be measured by the number of people reporting to you or the number of followers you have on Twitter. I have learned, I'm sure like many of you, that leadership is not some power that is bestowed; rather, you have to earn it and demonstrate it by your actions. Leadership is your ability to influence and persuade those around you, to act with a high degree of emotional intelligence, to use proper judgment, and to make the tough choices when no one is watching. Over the years I have learned a lot more from advisors about leadership than managers I reported to. These advisors didn't need the title because they were leaders from the start and they had sound principles and strong values.

> "Results are obtained by exploiting opportunities, not by solving problems."
>
> —*Peter Drucker*

New players moving into our industry should surprise no one. With nearly $17 trillion in investment assets in play and a compelling annual growth rate of 8.4 percent, wealth management is one of the most attractive sectors within financial services, especially in the high-net-worth space involving $57 trillion globally.

Even less surprising is that technology is yet again unleashing a tidal wave of change in our industry. Our smart, sophisticated clients are always looking to take advantage of new technology and new players.

Rising competition and the other top trends in wealth management have led to automated advisors, predictive analytics to enhance the client experience, financial planning and advice tools, and integrated wealth management experience, according to the management consulting corporation Capgemini.

Many people in our space see technology firms' interest in wealth management as a direct threat to the traditional investment advisory model—and rightly so. If our new competitors can deliver better service at a competitive cost, then why should our clients stay with us? We'd better have the answer. Finding the right solution may mean we need to redefine our value proposition and accept that we'll have to innovate and reinvest in the client experience if we are going to remain competitive. If you're not sure, ask yourself this: Can artificial intelligence replace what I'm doing in the near future? Can algorithms replace ultimate responsibility for portfolio management? Can software deliver solutions that replace me? This is not the future; this is now. We are living in a 140-character digital labor market. The future advisor will leverage digital labor and tools to create a better client experience and efficiencies and capture more market share. All we need to do is look around to see how brick-and-mortar is being replaced by digital, brick by brick and click by click.

Regardless of how big your book of business is today, your business model needs to evolve, including automating processes or outsourcing time-consuming tasks such as investment management. Leveraging new technologies in your business creates more scale and efficiency, leaving you more time to build and deepen relationships. Not only do we have an aging client population, but we have an aging advisor population as well. Therefore, it would be wise for any team to think about the next generation because they will inherit billions of dollars. This new base of clients, generation X and Y, will want a different client experience.

Technology will allow you to operate in real time through various channels. The time to start connecting to the next generation is now.

The Leadership Response

There is only one response to tackle these looming threats: leaders in the wealth management sector who embrace a growth mindset will continue to compete and outcompete the competition. In doing so, you will be prepared for anything that is thrown at you. There is a proverb in martial arts: "Master, why do you teach me to fight, but speak of peace?" The master replies, "It is better to be a warrior in a garden than a gardener in a war." If you believe that we are in a war to capture client assets, to retain those assets, and to retain top talent, then you will operate with a sense of purpose, urgency, and focus. You may be the peaceful warrior with a mental shield of armor, but you're ready for battle, ready to protect your business and grow. But how? You may need to invest in new technology to serve a segment of your business with a different value proposition and cost. You may need to drastically improve your value proposition and service model. You may need to closely evaluate your team to determine if their skill sets are outdated. You may need to be more diligent about client segmentation. You may need to re-evaluate your relationship with time. Are you spending it on high-payoff activities? You may need to think about a partnership or acquisition. You may need to work on yourself because your leadership skills—and specifically your people skills—are paramount. We are, above all else, in the people business: we are people who work with people. We need to stay on top of the technological innovations that are changing our industry. But more importantly, we need to continue to leverage skills such as emotional intelligence, creativity and collaboration.

> "While technology has eliminated many mid-level jobs, pay is going up for senior managers, because skills such as emotional intelligence, creative thinking and advanced judgment are in short supply."
>
> —*Korn Ferry, Executive Recruiters*

To put it even more simply, we need to continue to grow as leaders. In *The Growth Mindset*, I want to share with you the tools and insights that I've gained from examining what makes great leaders in our industry so that you can compete more effectively with anything and everything that evolving technologies—and other competition—may throw at you. Technology advances and regulatory changes over the past ten years have brought new transparency to the wealth management process. This means that the client has access to all the information they need. Trust, therefore, will have even greater significance. Transparency about fees, portfolio construction, or anything that may involve the advisor–client relationship is not only a necessity, but the next generation will demand even more transparency.

In my own career in wealth management, I have been influenced by a diverse group of leaders from different backgrounds, across a variety of cultures, with very different approaches to the business. I want to share these insights with you because in my work I see too many missed opportunities for leaders—opportunities to do the right thing, create value, and make a real difference in the lives of the people they lead and the investors they serve. Seizing these opportunities is critical and will only become more essential as technology continues to affect how wealth management services are delivered.

> "The world is more malleable than you think and it's waiting for you to hammer it into shape."
>
> —*Bono*

Over the course of my 34 years in the business, I have worked with about 42,000 wealth management advisors and managers in all channels—across wirehouses, Registered Investment Advisors (RIA), independent broker dealers, and bank trusts. I have worked with firms of 86,000 employees and firms of fewer than 25 employees and with managers and advisors from North America, Europe, the Middle East, Australia, and Asia. Each of these interactions had unique aspects—different structures, platforms, products, and services—deployed across different cultures.

Yet, one thing was consistent. One thing created business results. One thing made all the difference in people's lives: leadership. And successful leadership demands two things: one, they are brilliant in the fundamentals; and two, success is in execution. Success is never about being fancy with trying to achieve better results. Successful leaders achieve better results because they get the fundamentals right: the culture, the vision, strategies, and the right people in the right roles.

I'm referring to a very specific kind of leadership—what I call *growth mindset leadership*.

The Five Types of Managers

Based on my experience crisscrossing the country, I see five types of managers in the wealth management industry. By the way, the manager I'm referring to can be the one managing an organization of 20,000 employees or one of 3 employees. The academic community has created their own set of manager types and there are thousands of books describing these manager types in detail. Regardless of whether you are a team leader, a branch manager, a market manager, a divisional manager, a partner, a CEO at an RIA, or a CEO of a large firm, you are one of these types of leaders in my book:

- A growth mindset leader
- An administrator
- A command-and-control leader
- A laissez-faire manager
- A victim

If you are going to lead with certainty and conviction during this era of innovation, you will need to enhance the growth mindset leadership qualities in yourself, and this book will show you how. These proven principles are based on my 34 years of grit, hustle, hard work, and perseverance—qualities that took me all over the world to the most successful wealth management firms on the planet, where I observed firsthand what I now call the *growth mindset leader* in action. The leader as *administrator* is in self-preservation mode most of time and enjoys doing busy work; he is focused on playing it safe and never challenging the status quo. The *command-and-control* leader rules with an iron fist and feeds off of power and control; bullies typically like this model, while the *laissez-faire* leader is more interested in being everyone's friend. The leader as *victim* doesn't take responsibility. The victim blames other people and doesn't have the courage to do the right thing. The victim plays outside the arena and is quick to judge and point fingers. Victims are the negative leaders and are the most destructive to any organization.

True mastery in any discipline, including leadership, comes with focus, curiosity, discipline, knowledge, patience, time, and practice. Though there are no guarantees, I can promise these concepts will start the leadership flywheel both within your organization and within yourself. Take it from me—it won't be easy. If you are new to a leadership role, you'll need to be introspective and have a strong desire to want to make a difference. And if you have been in a leadership role for a long time, I hope some of these ideas will make a difference in your life and the lives of your team members and clients.

As you consider what type of leader you want to be and embrace growth mindset leadership, my advice is that you open your mind to new ideas and approaches. Specifically, I hope you approach the information and use the tools in this book as follows:

- Read with an open mind. It's the only way to grow and continue to add value.
- Look for what resonates with you and start trying something new. Take notes and mark up the margins.
- Consider how each principle or suggested action can be applied to your practice.

- Pay attention to your belief system in order not to quickly dismiss an idea.
- Do it.

"I hear and I forget. I see and I remember. I do and I understand."

—*Confucius*

What Is a Growth Mindset?

A growth mindset leader evolves, leads, and serves. As a friend of mine said recently, "I need to feel when I get up every morning that I'm growing." A growth mindset assumes that continued growth and improvement is possible. People with a growth mindset take full responsibility for their lives. They believe that with the right motivation and skills, anyone's true potential is virtually unlimited. It doesn't take long to recognize someone who is living with this mindset. People with this mindset have a sense of curiosity; they are open to possibilities, they have a positive outlook, and they have a desire to learn and make a difference. In short, a growth mindset promotes continued growth personally and professionally.

Most advisors plateau after 10 years. (The term *advisor* as used throughout this book refers, inclusively, to financial advisors, portfolio managers, relationship managers, trust advisors, and business development professionals.) They worked hard during those 10 years to reach a point where they are comfortable financially. After all this hard work, they want to reap the fruits of their labor and coast. They believe they have mastered all there is to learn about the business and go on cruise control. I call this group *cruisers*. That is not a mindset in growth mode, rather a mindset that plays it safe. Such a mindset will ultimately atrophy. Conversely, people who embody the growth mindset are always trying to reach their full potential, are creative and engaging. They are always stretching to find better ways to serve their clients. A growth mindset person is always looking for a new challenge. They always keep hope alive and never give up. By the way, if you're a cruiser, it's okay; I'm not here to judge. But you're reading this book for a reason and I hope you'll embrace some of the components of what it takes to be a growth mindset leader.

Over the past 25 years, I have been obsessed with understanding what makes some people successful and why others seem to just lose their way or never develop the right discipline, or how some people move from being a victim to having a different attitude and taking control of their business or life. From the beginning, as a young advisor trying to grow my business without a strong training program to take advantage of, I made it a daily habit to ask questions and watch what successful advisors did every day. I learned quickly that these advisors were focused on achieving their goals and were relentless in protecting their clients. They were different and the way they looked at the business was different. They enjoyed competing. They had a different belief system—a belief that it's not only what happens to you, but how you react to what happens. I believe that hard work and deeds will separate strong leaders from the pack. Most important, they were incredibly resilient. Market corrections, losing an important client relationship, changing management, and personal setbacks—nothing held them back. They moved forward regardless. They learned from their experiences and continued to learn and grow. They had a growth mindset.

As a young 23-year-old advisor, I didn't have a rich uncle to get me started in the business like some of my friends did. The only way I knew how to build a business—the way I was told to do it—was by making cold calls. And so I did, and my business grew slowly. I enjoyed the challenge of turning a "no" into a "yes." I always liked talking to people and still do today. I was always hustling and networking, which is not a dirty word in my book. People who hustle have energy and are alert. I was determined to make it in the business. I worked most Saturdays for the first 15 years and late nights 3 days a week for 25 years. Weekends were also spent catching up on reading research reports, annual reports, books, and *Barron's*. I also enjoyed listening to audio books while driving to work, and today I download them on my iPad.

My coaches and teachers helped me develop my own growth mindset in high school. My football, wrestling, and track coaches made me believe that if I worked hard and dedicated myself and most of all persevered, anything is possible. Thanks to my teammates and coaches, I went on to be an all-state running back. I learned the power of teamwork and always keeping your ego in check. As I moved into the wealth management industry, I knew quickly that without the help of mentors it would be much more challenging. Therefore, I was on the lookout for those that could play that role. And they likewise told me that if I worked hard enough, built a foundation of knowledge, and broadened my mind, I would be successful. My early mentors taught me several valuable lessons that still serve me well.

Don't waste your time saying "It's not fair," because life doesn't care how you feel. Take responsibility if you want something. Be honest with yourself and others. "It's not my fault" didn't exist among our teammates; you are one hundred percent accountable.

A common theme throughout this book is to live your life on your terms; that means designing a business model that gets you excited to get up every morning and gives you a meaningful purpose. To the older advisors, I hope this book inspires you to take on a new challenge, bring on and mentor a younger advisor, and take your business to the next level because you can change your cruise control setting.

The focus throughout this book will be on the soft skills, the vision, communicating effectively, the future wealth management model, attracting the high-net-worth client and building client loyalty, and recruiting, coaching and creating great teams. Investment management is important and there's an ocean of books on the market. Because after all, the advisor is the real solution and not the products or platform. The real differentiation is the advisor.

My passion for helping people who are motivated to grow started a long time ago. Watching people stretch to reach for something they care about is inspiring. After three decades of running businesses, coaching, and speaking, I'm still moved when someone who has been in the business for 40 or 50 years comes to one of my workshops simply because he or she still has a strong sense of curiosity or because he or she wants to possibly learn something new to be able to serve their clients better. These people have a growth mindset in and out of the office, professionally and personally. They live their abundant lives with enthusiasm. If you hang around them long enough, that mindset is contagious. This book will give you a roadmap to take your business to the next level. And it all starts with purpose, vision, and a growth mindset.

Wealth Management Success Model

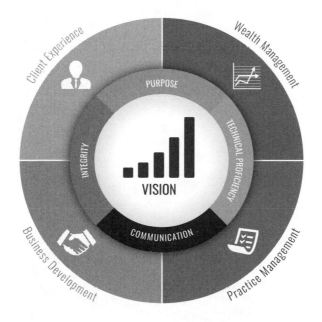

Based on my experience, the success model needs to have two characteristics: business characteristics and personal characteristics. The business components are wealth management, practice management, business development, and client experience. The personal characteristics are purpose, technical proficiency, communication, and integrity. The book is built around this model. Everything starts with a vision. The advisor that embraces change and adapts to the new realities will have a competitive advantage. *The Economist*, January 14, 2017, issue cover and special report "Lifelong Learning" on how to survive in the age of automation describes how in many occupations, it has become essential to acquire new skills. Wealth Management is no exception and requires financial advisors to continuously reboot.

Acknowledgments

This book is a result of a lifetime of learning, thinking, talking, reading, and most of all working with many great leaders on getting better business results. At the core I have been a student of human performance since I graduated from college. And over the past three decades I have been playing in the arena of Wall Street with some wins, some losses, and my share of mistakes. The battle scars to inch out the competition made all of us improve our game. When I look back, I can gain perspective and reflect on the people who had an impact in my life and helped me shape my philosophy on human potential and growing a wealth management business. Writing a book is a massive undertaking and for the most part very enjoyable, but I'm not rushing to write another book anytime soon. One of the challenges of writing a book is the fact that any author wants to produce the very best piece of work;

therefore, I tried to pay attention to the smallest details. But I never totally got comfortable letting go and saying to myself I'm done. Just like painting a landscape, even years after it's done, you feel one more brushstroke could make a difference. Therefore I'm sure I edited out 30,000 words before all was said and done. Though writing is a solitary activity and a nice change from speaking in front of a large group, I must confess I'd much rather be with a group of growth-minded leaders talking about life and business than in my office typing away and doing research. The right people give me energy and ideas and are inspiring. I'll admit that as a professional speaker my mind is always on the lookout for ways to be more effective and persuasive.

One of the best parts of writing this book was the opportunity to meet leaders I haven't met before and reconnecting with old friends. I am grateful to my family and friends for their support and candid feedback and always making sure my feet are firmly planted on the ground. Thanks to my daughters, Bianca and Emilia. They create a deep joy in my life and I'm so grateful that we can share a life together. To my brother, Egidio, and my sister, Giovanna, for always being there for me. To my wife, Barbara, for always supporting my adventures and dreams.

I am grateful to all the advisors I have worked with over the years. This book would not have been possible without their friendship, support, and ideas. I am indebted to my friends who provided feedback and support, including Bob Dunwoody, Joe Grano, Jim Carbonaro, Tim Ursiny, Alex Murray, Jonathan Cressy, Rafer Kingston, John Christiana, Tina Powell, Kevin Sincavage, John H. Decker, Cary Greenspan, Sid Queler, Mark Casady, Dave Kelly,

Courtney McQuade, Craig Pfeiffer, Lisa Carnoy, Rich Dragotta, Tony Davidow, John Hyland, Ira Wolfe, Stacey Glemboski and Jennifer Skancke. Thank you as well to the team at Wiley, who provided top-notch support and guidance, including Julie Kerr, Michael Henton, Gayathri Govindarajan, Judy Howarth, Bill Falloon, and Shelley Flannery.

Finally, I beg forgiveness of all those who have played a role in helping me with this book over the past year but whose names I have failed to mention.

PART ONE

Leadership Makes a Difference in Wealth Management

Leadership is the buzzword of the twenty-first century. Who is a leader? What qualities do the best leaders have? Are leaders born or made? It's a bull market for leadership books, and that should not surprise us. Because of the increasing rate of change in the marketplace we are looking for ways to adapt, improve, and increase performance. With over 20,000 books on leadership available, it's difficult to come across a new idea that the great thinkers and philosophers have not written about in the past 2,400 years. Therefore, I'm not trying to reinvent the wheel; I'm simply trying to share the proven leadership strategies that achieve business results. These strategies are

1

based on research and my own experience over the past 34 years. These ideas are not based on consulting assignments; they are based on my street-tested strategies and tactics working side by side with advisors, managers, and clients.

Within the wealth management industry, these questions about leadership are critically important as the industry overall is undergoing a revolution. In situations where advisors traditionally make recommendations and act (or not) based on their clients' responses, today's successful wealth management requires strong leadership to build client relationships and construct full wealth management plans to achieve the life goals of clients. Today, an advisor must be a leader. It is nonnegotiable.

Let's look at it from the history of humankind and how we survived and evolved over the years. For millions of years, humans lived as hunter-gatherers. Then humans shifted to farming for thousands of years, then to the age of industry for hundreds of years, and then to the Information Age for several decades. And the next age upon us is the age of augmentation. Each shift has happened faster than the one before it. Our ability to evolve with each new phase requires strong leaders to learn and adapt faster than they have had to in the past.

Part One of this book focuses on identifying and defining the leadership qualities you need to set yourself apart from the 300,000 advisors in the United States. From communication to collaboration, from creating a vision to establishing a culture, from recruiting to coaching, and from courage to empowerment and gratitude, these are just some of the leadership topics covered in these chapters. The chapters I cover in Part One are based on my observations for the past three decades of what the most effective leaders have done to achieve success and what they are doing today to grow a wealth management business. The overall theme revolves around delivering a truly holistic, consultative and customized solution for the high-net-worth client. I emphasize the importance of creating deeper relationships versus focusing on transactions. Leveraging new technologies in your business creates more scale and efficiency, leaving you more time to build and deepen relationships. You may need to reevaluate your relationships with people in your life and on your team. Critical to this process is making sure that you are taking care of yourself. The focus is on the soft skills and that internal dialogue. It's about our belief system and the demons that we are trying to shake off and rise above.

Just as we approach the client relationship holistically we will approach the advisor's relationship the same way. Over the years I have seen tactical business plans that simply don't have staying power because the plan lacks vision, purpose, and strategy. Many advisors simply keep doing the same things and expecting different results. These qualities are becoming more critical than ever because the advice business is changing right in front of us. The historic purview was narrowly focused around investment solutions. The future of advice needs to be much broader in scope and depth. It needs to include discussion of liabilities, tax and estate planning, insurance needs, healthcare planning, assistance with budgeting and spending controls, cash flow analysis, and legacy planning. The past was about seeking alpha returns and that was the differentiator for choosing one wealth manager over another. The future will be about helping clients achieve their goals—all of their goals.

Therefore, the right leadership will set the right vision and strategy to evolve to these changing needs and take market share.

Chapter 1

Communicate Effectively to Move People to Action

"The most important thing in communication is hearing what isn't said."

—Peter Drucker

Growth is impossible without communication and leaders with a growth mindset are great communicators. This means that they are great listeners as well as compelling storytellers. Your ability to master the art of communication is your greatest tool. How do we influence and persuade others? We use our position, authority, experience, skill, and knowledge. All very important to be effective, however this is only half of the equation; this is where many miss the opportunity to be great communicators. They forget, or don't understand, that just as important is not only what we say, but how, when, and where we say it. Your gestures, timing, tone, rhythm, and overall body language. Once you truly understand that you are always communicating, not just when you open your mouth, you have a better opportunity to be effective. Focus more energy on how you say it. Our ability to sell ourselves and our ideas is paramount to be successful in wealth management.

Listen to Understand

Leadership is not a monologue—it's a dialogue. It's about asking compelling questions and then listening—really listening—to the answers. Great leaders are intuitive listeners who can quickly size up the emotional needs of others and respond appropriately. They can establish rapport very quickly. They have big antennas in order to identify common interests and are able to make emotional connections. If you have been in the business for some time, I'm sure you are saying to yourself, but of course communication is important, this is basic. Yes, it's basic and yes, everyone knows this. So why do I bring it up in the first chapter? While the majority of managers and advisors agree that communication is critical to the business, I'm amazed by how many are unable to communicate effectively. Our words say one thing and our body language says something different. People don't think before they speak and then it comes out the wrong way. People are misunderstood all the time because the advisor or manager didn't take the time to listen or never learned how to listen actively and intuitively. Today, technology makes it so easy to send a text message or email, but we are in the people business. I can learn more from looking into someone's eyes after I ask them a question than I can from an exchange of 20 emails. That's why I call communication an art, and that's why I'm suggesting, based on thousands of client meetings and seeing people's personal interactions, that *we can improve*. It's simply the most effective tool. To understand and be understood is a wonderful thing when it happens. It's about mastering the fundamentals.

First, most of the time we make assumptions of what people really mean when we hear them. Everything people say is open for interpretation. For example, if I say to you, "Bob, that's an interesting tie you have on," 99 percent of the time when I make this statement in my workshops, I get the same response, "Thank you." I didn't say I liked the tie; I didn't say I didn't like the tie; therefore what did I say? Nothing. A better response might be, "What do you mean by 'it's an interesting tie'?" If a prospect says, "I'm risk averse," we can't reply by simply saying "Okay." The better response is, "Please tell me more about that," or "What do you mean?" The point is, it's imperative we stop making assumptions or misinterpreting what clients are saying. This can only happen if we slow down a lot. Stop talking and instead peel the onion back by asking follow-up questions.

Ask yourself:
- Do I listen when others talk or just focus on my response?
- Am I focused on the speaker or am I thinking about what I need to do next?

- How well am I picking up and listening to what is *not* being said?
- How well am I reading their body language?

"When people talk, listen completely."

—*Ernest Hemingway*

Talk to Be Understood

Great leaders communicate clearly, expressing themselves in a way that's authentic and doesn't keep people guessing. A leader talks to help people understand the big picture, get inspired, and execute on a shared vision.

The win-win model I follow for an effective meeting includes having a clear vision of the ultimate objective, doing your homework, understanding the purpose of this particular meeting, asking Socratic questions, discovering what you can do for the person you're meeting with, meeting in a location to foster the most productive atmosphere, and following up on next steps. We both know how many meetings take place every day around the country with a small group or hundreds without a clear objective or action steps or being inspired because the leader was a poor communicator.

Consider this:

- Become a great storyteller. Storytelling has been ingrained in our DNA since the first humans sat around a fire sharing stories. People never forget a good

WIN-WIN

ASK

story. Use vivid descriptions, metaphors, and analogies. Evoke powerful emotions. A master storyteller understands his audience, whether it consists of one person or one thousand. The next generation will respond well to visual storytelling.

- Know how to keep it pithy. Less is often more.
- Note that being a storyteller is different from being a spin doctor. Spin doctors are never credible. Authentic storytellers are more than credible. They are inspiring.

Whether talking or writing, keep it simple. We're all dealing with information overload in a challenging business. Don't make anything more difficult or complicated than it needs to be. Being an effective communicator takes time and practice. It doesn't just happen. Watch great communicators on YouTube or TED Talks. One of the best in the business is Charlie Rose. He does his homework, asks smart questions, and lets the person talk, all of which makes him a great listener and communicator. If you want to be a better communicator, start paying attention to how you communicate and be determined to improve. If you're not sure, video yourself using your phone. I *guarantee* that you will always find something you can improve on.

An Outstanding Communicator

I have been privileged to work with some exceptional leaders over the years, many of whom are incredibly skilled communicators. Standing out in that phenomenal crowd is the former CEO of UBS, Joe Grano—a friend of mine and one of the best leaders in the business.

Joe came to Paine Webber (now UBS) when performance, morale, and everything else at the company was hitting rock-bottom. He showed his mettle in every situation. In fact, the greater the crisis, the calmer Joe became. He gave you the feeling that everything was going to work out. He always communicated with full transparency and authenticity.

Once, at a chairman's club meeting of about 400 top advisors, he announced a compensation adjustment, telling advisors that if they wanted to earn what they earned last year, they would need to be more productive. Every other CEO or head of a similar group would have been met with a roomful of silence at best or more likely some pretty loud feedback.

Joe received a standing ovation. He is the only person I know who would get that reaction. What was Joe's secret?

He was always honest with people, he did not spin the facts, he cared about you, and he was inspirational. He spoke from his heart and took personal risks to do the right thing.

You knew Joe had your back. In return, people would go through a brick wall for him, including me. He made us feel that we were in this together—we were partners.

I'll give you an even clearer sense of how much Joe cared about people. When my mother died, I was devastated and traumatized. My mother was my mentor and best friend. Joe took the time to talk to me about his own experience with grief and gave me his support and advice. He followed up with a long handwritten letter that was so moving and contained so much compassion that I can honestly say that his words were the only ones that gave me any comfort. Joe had the ability to empathize with people.

Joe is a special person and a great communicator.

Sales Meeting: Great Leaders Don't Waste Anyone's Time

Being prepared and organized leads to efficient communication. Leaders with a growth mindset value their time and the time of others. As a leader, running an efficient meeting directly contributes to your credibility and effectiveness. Every meeting is an opportunity to have an impact. If you just wing it, it will show. That's why only 20 percent of advisors report that meetings are a worthwhile use of their time. Here are some crucial points to consider for creating a well-organized, impactful strategy meeting or sales meeting:

- Always have an agenda. Invest time in preparing for every meeting.
- Spend some time reviewing the minutes from the previous meeting.

- Make appropriate announcements and give a brief introduction of the topics that will be covered during the meeting.
- Give an update of how your office and the market is performing: the good, the bad, and the ugly.
- Regularly schedule meetings and always start and end on time.
- Have handouts and always have a few advisors share their ideas.
- Consider featuring an outside guest speaker every week.
- Ask for feedback after the meeting from the participants.
- Show strong leadership during and after the meeting.
- Be very specific what you want people to do and why.
- Always take the opportunity to recognize the right behavior and the results being achieved.
- Reinforce the culture you are trying to build.

Important: Coach your advisors on what they will talk about. Ensure they focus on the key points. Limit each speaker to five minutes.

Important: Be sincere and prepare yourself, because the truth can hurt. When you ask for feedback, you will hear the good and bad. I made adjustments to how I ran my meetings all the time. I wanted people to look forward to these meetings, so I knew I had to tailor my presentations to accommodate what worked and eliminate what didn't. I wanted the participants to walk away with a few good actionable ideas from the meeting that they could use not only to grow their book, but also to better service the client.

Don't make the mistake of raising a negative subject because you want to send a message to a few people. That's a waste of time for the other 48 people in the room. Talk to those few people separately.

Follow-up: Thank-You Notes Are Magic

After every meeting, send handwritten notes to the guest speaker and to any advisor who spoke. A simple thank-you note will let them know that they did a nice job and that you appreciate them. It may seem old-school to do this, but it makes a huge impact and impression. It's a personal touch that never goes unnoticed.

Winning Hearts and Minds

How can you coach an advisor on better client connectivity, building trust faster, and establishing rapport if you have not mastered the art of communication?

Since I now make my living as a professional speaker, I'll give you my top pointers:

1. We are in the business of winning hearts and minds. I always start with the emotional side, the heart. I focus on body language and anything that gives me clues into the heart of the person I am speaking with. My antenna is always up, and I'm looking to connect whether it's one-on-one or with a group of 1,000.

2. Develop a level of intimacy that makes each individual in the room feel as if you're speaking directly to him or her. Putting politics aside, Bill Clinton and Oprah Winfrey do this extraordinarily well.

3. Great communicators read their audience carefully to ensure they can connect quickly. Always make sure

you understand who your audience is before you open your mouth. Try not to adjust your message on the fly, but if you need to, be sure to stay on message.

4. I make myself fully transparent and am authentic. Never underestimate how smart your audience is and how fast they can pick up if you're not being honest or authentic.

5. I use my energy to give energy and in return start feeding off that energy. Any strength overextended becomes a weakness. Therefore, don't focus too much energy on trying to be liked. That's an amateur mistake in public speaking. Be yourself and study great public speakers.

6. I go over a presentation in my head many times before I go on stage. I get into a state of flow—in the zone—and nothing gets in my way. I also avoid negative people as much as I can especially before a presentation.

7. Use examples and metaphors to make your point. Tackle complex ideas and deliver them in a simple, understandable way.

8. Start with the end in mind: What do you want people to say about you and your presentation? I like people to say, "Rick was authentic, he didn't spin anything, he was inspiring, he was empowering." Select the words that you want people to say before you start building your presentation.

9. I never start talking about what I don't know well and I never pretend to know something I don't. I'm perfectly fine saying, "I don't know."

10. I never use sarcasm, politics, or religion in my presentations. I'm always respectful of the people in the audience and don't assume to know their background

or personal histories. I never engage in an argument. Because most of the time those people who initiate an argument are victims just trying to prove to others how smart they are. It's a waste of time and it will derail you.

Inspiration: Lead by Example

"You must be the change you want to see in the world."
—*Mahatma Gandhi*

An effective communicator can inspire people to take action. But of course the best way to inspire people is to speak from the heart with clarity and passion, and then lead by example. Walking the talk is not something we see every day.

Almost anyone can be a peacetime general. It's when times get tough that the mettle of true leadership is revealed. When you're emotionally knocked down, you still need to be seen and heard as a leader and you need to use good judgment and execute tough decisions.

"Great leaders move us. They ignite our passion and inspire the best in us. When we try to explain why they are so effective, we speak of strategy, vision, or powerful ideas. But the reality is much more primal. Great leadership works through the emotions."
—*Daniel Goleman, Primal Leadership*

Ask yourself:
- How do I perform under stress?
- How well do I communicate our vision?
- How well do I inspire others to achieve their goals?
- What do I need to be inspired?

If you signed up to be a leader, you have signed up to lead the way from the front—to be a role model. That means you have the responsibility to meet or exceed the high standard you'd like to set for your people whether it's three people or 3,000. You're accountable 24/7 and you need to be willing to do whatever you ask others to do. If you tend to avoid client appointments because you have other things to do, I would strongly suggest that you meet with clients on a regular basis. I don't care if you are the CEO of the largest firm in the world. Meeting with clients is a must for anyone in the executive office. No one should hide behind the curtain and make decisions without the firsthand knowledge of the present circumstances that it takes to win a client relationship. I meet with hundreds of senior leaders a year and I often ask them two questions: How often do you meet with clients? and How much time do you spend coaching or mentoring others? Their response gives me many clues into their leadership style.

There's no leadership strategy more powerful or effective than leading by example. How you treat people, how you recognize people, how you react to criticism, how you treat the client—how you act in every situation—are all critical elements that contribute to the effectiveness of your leadership. The bottom line is you should be willing to do anything yourself that you are asking your team to do.

> "What you *do* speaks so loudly that I cannot hear what you say."
>
> —*Ralph Waldo Emerson*

Ask yourself:
- Do I walk the talk?
- Do I ask people to be punctual—but am habitually late for meetings?

- Do I coach people to listen more effectively and actively, to their clients—but don't listen to my advisors when they talk?
- Do I talk about respect—but am rude to the organization's maintenance staff?
- If someone followed me around with a camera 24 hours a day, would I behave differently?
- Am I telling people what to do or am I showing them?

Inspire Others and Yourself

An inspired leader moves people to action. For me, this is the biggest difference between a good manager and a great manager or an average advisor and an elite advisor. A good manager has a to-do list. A great leader inspires others to take action through their own words and actions. Communication is not just about what we say. In fact, how, why, and where we say it is often more important. Being a genuine, effective, and inspired communicator means you feel good about yourself and you have a healthy balance of confidence, which is naturally inspiring to others.

You cannot inspire others if you're not inspired yourself. Motivation is an external state; inspiration is internal. As you cultivate self-awareness, inspiration becomes your way of life and your way of moving around. As a result, you will gain a clearer sense of your professional and personal purpose.

When you're inspired, you inspire others. People who are inspiring exude positive energy. They don't need to say much: we feel their energy. It affects us in a positive way. The reverse is true when we are around people who are uninspiring. We feel their negative energy and it brings us down. That's why when an effective leader visits a location he makes an effort to walk around and connect with people. And if a leader doesn't do that, it may mean he doesn't want to hear any complaints or simply believes he has higher priorities. If you're the leader, you have an obligation to connect to your team.

Don't get me wrong: being inspired doesn't mean subsisting on a daily dose of quotes or music or someone to pump you up. There will be times when you don't feel inspired and you aren't able to inspire your people. Don't fake it. There's no need to, and people see right through it, anyway. Because some days you're thrown a curve ball. Because as you know it takes resilience to be able to deal with everything that wealth management throws at you, not to mention life. Today, I'm inspired by people all the time. Nature is my daily inspiration and living with gratitude helps me live a more balanced life.

If you're a professional, the show goes on. Every Sunday when a football player steps onto the field the fans don't care what happened to the player on Saturday. What matters is long-term performance and the core philosophy that underpins it. If you work at getting inspired and staying inspired, you will operate at a more effective level most of the time and you will be able to inspire people around you, through your example, over the long haul. I have had to develop the discipline to inspire others (when I give a presentation) even when I just received bad news about something. Being able to compartmentalize these feelings is important. When people show up from around the country to hear me speak, I need to bring my best game. They don't care what happened to me one hour before I get on stage. People don't care about *why* you are not fully prepared for a client meeting; they just know that you aren't prepared.

Consider this:
- Get inspired: find positive energy for yourself and others because you cannot give away what you don't have.
- Take a class, read a book, and challenge yourself with difficult questions.
- Learn something new. Put yourself out of your comfort zone.

Reward Yourself and Your Team

Inspiring yourself is also about creating the right set of personal and professional challenges that keep you motivated and operating in the optimal zone. You need short- and long-term goals and you must reward yourself when you achieve certain milestones. A reward doesn't have to be an expensive gift; it could be an event or activity or something else. Think of creative and motivational ways to reward yourself or someone you care about at least once a month. When I was a young advisor and I had a successful month or week, I would stop by my favorite florist and buy my mother flowers. She loved flowers, and when I walked into the kitchen to give them to her, the smile on her face lit up the room. Do the same for your team. Great leaders reward themselves and others.

"Leadership is not magnetic personality, that can just as well be a glib tongue. It is not 'making friends and influencing people,' that is flattery. Leadership is lifting a person's vision to higher sights, the raising of a person's performance to a higher standard, the building of a personality beyond its normal limitations."

—*Peter Drucker, Management: Tasks, Responsibilities, Practices*

Chapter 2

Create a Compelling Vision

"Whatever you do, or dream you can, begin it. Boldness has genius, magic and power in it."

—*Goethe*

Inspired leaders lead with long-term visions for their teams and organizations. A shared vision is how a leader creates a committed and invested team. We all know that advisors in general are mostly focused on their practice only. They mainly care about their clients, themselves, and their family. So why are we talking about having a vision? Because almost everyone would like to be part of a winning team and be part of a community of people with shared principles and values. People want to know that others around them are also committed to excellence and that the team, division, or firm has a vision. Where are we going? How will we get there and why are we doing this?

21

Before you can create a vision for your team or firm, you need to become very clear about your personal vision, your values, and your principles. You need to answer the question, "How will everyone benefit if we achieve this vision?"

Vision needs to be shared. As an advisor you need to start with your vision. It could be the vision of a small wealth management team of three, a partnership, or the executive office. But whoever the stakeholders are—*everyone* must be committed to that vision for it to stand a chance of becoming fulfilled.

Until you truly believe and envision what your business, team, office, region, or firm should be, you're sailing without a rudder. You will likely create confusion and the lack of motivation will be pervasive. Based on my personal research and experience, most firms or teams operate without a clear vision. And, if there is only one person in the organization who can describe the vision, chances are it is the person who created it. The firms that have a clear vision operate with a sense of purpose. These types of firms or teams occur quite infrequently. The following is an example of what commonly happens across firms without a vision. A firm I worked with a few years ago had gone through major organizational changes over several years and the new CEO felt the firm had gone through so much upheaval that it was best to default to doing nothing. In other words, his mindset was that people couldn't handle more disruption, and therefore it was best not to do anything to cause more upheaval. Even though he was the new CEO of the firm, he never created a new vision nor did he ever talk about how the firm would not only compete but win under his leadership.

As a result, everyone became confused about the future, who they were as an organization, what the new organizational culture would be, and how they would achieve their objectives and serve their clients. As I mentioned earlier, this tends to be the norm in many companies that have undergone a lot of leadership change.

By the way, you don't need to have a large firm to have a vision. It doesn't matter if you are one advisor or a three-person team, having a vision is important. It will serve as the lighthouse, the North Star.

Consider this:

1. Create a clear and vivid picture of where you want to go, why you want to go there, what "there" looks like, and why anyone should care about it.
2. Set out *how* you are going to get there.

The future is unknown, the markets are unknown, and change is constant. Your vision should focus on the people inside the organization, as well as the value you're committed to creating for clients. Be enthusiastic and energetic about the future. A vision is an act of creation.

Ask yourself:

- How does our vision benefit the client and the people on our team?

A business vision is not about you; it's about the people you serve. Every decision you make about the future should have the client front and center. Every decision should be guided by these questions:

- How does our vision benefit the client?
- How does our vision benefit the back office?

- How does our vision benefit the front office?
- How does our vision benefit the community?
- How does our vision benefit the shareholders?

Growth Is a Choice

Let me stress again that before you create a team vision or a corporate vision, you have to cultivate self-awareness and create your own personal vision. You may be asking why I am making such a big deal about having a personal vision. Vision is all about authenticity and the quest for authenticity starts with self-awareness.

Since 2008, I have called my advisor and manager training and consulting programs, which are designed to grow assets under management and evolve overall wealth management practices, "Growth Is a Choice." The reason for that title is simple: everyone has the power to create his or her own vision. Everyone has the power to choose growth over fear or over complacency. We can either design a life starting with an intentional vision or we can react aimlessly to everything that comes our way. We can be the creator of our destiny or a victim of circumstances.

The choice is ours.

Consider this:
- The only thing you *must do* to live is maintain a body temperature of 98.6 degrees. Everything else in your life is your choice and part of your vision. You have the power to make decisions that will help you and others live a more purposeful life. Let me say it again: everyone

has the power to choose growth over fear or over complacency. We will talk more about Be + Do = Have in Chapter 23. Your personal vision is the "Be" part of the equation. You dramatically increase your odds of achieving success once you know who you like to "Be" and only then you will start doing the activities necessary to achieve your objectives.

All it takes is courage and discipline.

"The best way to predict the future is to create it."

—*Abraham Lincoln*

I have known Mark Casady for a number of years and knew he would have great insights on successful leadership practices. Mark is smart and driven and has incredible communication skills. He has a wonderful combination of emotional intelligence and practical business acumen. Unlike some CEOs with inflated egos, Mark is humble and has a good handle on what's important in life, especially as he retires from LPL Financial and is spending more time traveling and engaging in entrepreneurial ventures, which he calls life 2.0—the next version of his life.

Rick: Mark, how did you get started in the business?

Mark: I loved the markets and always thought I would be a portfolio manager. I went to work for Northern Trust in 1982 and they had this wonderful training program. I realized quickly you can buy a company as a portfolio manager but you couldn't change the company itself. I like IBM, or I don't like IBM, but you couldn't fix it, and that was incredibly frustrating to me.

Rick: When did you join LPL?

Mark: I joined in 2002 as the COO with about 4,000 advisors. I became president in 2003 and in 2004 I became CEO. Over 12 years LPL grew from about 5,000 advisors to 14,000, with another 4,000 affiliated with AXA for a total of 18,000. About 20 percent was acquisitions and the rest was organic. We went from $90 billion in assets to about $500 billion in that same time frame.

Rick: How did all the stars line up to achieve this kind of success?

Mark: We started with smaller advisors and went up the market over the years. It was a time of a lot of accumulation of assets by the investment community. The second wave we rode was consolidation and I believe we will see more consolidation over the next two to three years. The third was the march to independence and it continues today. We built out new capabilities, financial planning, and rebalancing tools. We tried to respond to the advisor needs.

Rick: How do you see the future of independent broker dealers in terms of margin compression?

Mark: Advisors will have more options—everyone will feel compression. Self-clearing makes a big difference. If we didn't self-clear, we would have a third of the margin we have. We control custody and control cost. Multi-custodians are almost free today, and it will not always be that way. These custodians are saying if you give me $300 million it will be one price, but if you give me $1 billion it will be this price. You need to have someone that's your major partner.

Rick: What advice would you give an advisor who's interested in growing the business?

Mark: They need to do three things differently: First, they need to change the dialogue from "I manage your money" and "This is the expected return" to "I help you figure out what money means to you." Most of the problems for consumers are due to behavior and not a problem with the portfolio. We all came into the business because we love markets. "Hey, Rick, I'm smarter than everyone else, come and work with me." And that's a nice pitch. The problem is I'm selling you a commodity, which is a return. Compare that to "Hey, Rick, let's talk about what you want to do with your money, and what your money is going to mean to you." The advisors need to get into the client's head. Why do you spend so much? What's your relationship with money? You have to have the mind of a capitalist in terms of how markets work and the heart of a social worker. The problem I see is that we spend too much time on the capital market side and not enough on the soft side, the relationship-building side. The best advisors I talk to tell me they spend a lot more time on the soft skills.

The second thing is they need to automate the process by outsourcing as much as they can, including rebalancing, social media, portfolio modeling. The practices that are growing faster are those that use a standardized approach. Because, guess what? This frees up the advisors to spend time on building relationships. So they need to get efficient.

The third thing that needs to change is to outsource investment management. You will not be able to afford the talent it takes to run a portfolio. Now you need to be able to talk about markets and you need to understand who you outsourced to and know if they are doing a good job. So you need to be able to evaluate performance, but that's a different skill.

Rick: What does it take to be an effective leader in the wealth management business?

Mark: I would ask advisors: What's the brand experience you are trying to create? What's the look and feel for the client? How do we interact with the client? You need to define what it means to have a great experience for the client.

The second is how do we make money? It doesn't matter if you're at the wirehouse, bank trust, or independent. This question gets to the heart of your strategic vision and value proposition. For me it's a clear way to get to the point of why we are in business.

Rick: How do you think the advice business will be disrupted by technology?

Mark: I don't think technology will displace the advisor if they evolve to the new world. The issue is cost. Robots will not take over the world. The next generation will still want face-to-face. When I have a little bit of money, I have a gambling pool and I can open an account online and trade. When they accumulate more assets, they will seek advice from a human being. The big issue is cost. What's the right price to pay? When we look at fintech, which is my new life, we look for technology that lowers costs and produces better outcomes. The mass affluent market will expand because of robos because in the past this group didn't get any advice. The advisor can use robo solutions for a certain segment of their book. The trend that's real is this cost trend, so this cost is also driven down because of lower investment returns over time and market volatility. Therefore, it's going to impact the cost you pay. That's why ETFs are so popular, and robos that do asset allocation at a reduced cost from 100 basis points to 35.

Rick: What advice would you give an active asset manager?

Mark: Great question. I was just asked this question by a big firm in town [Boston]. This model has not changed in 30 years and it's wrong. It's really very simple to me; you have to lower costs. The only question is, how do you do that so it doesn't destroy your existing business? Close the old fund and open a new fund with new pricing and you may need less wholesale force. A wholesaler just going around selling a product doesn't get much attention. They have to show how they add value to the practice. Some asset managers do this better than others. To me this is the best example of how wholesalers add value by helping the advisors grow their business. They walk in and they can help you with robo advice, risk management tools, and practice management. They can help you with a whole range of things that go well beyond the product conversation. The value-add wholesaling will be key going forward. I think we will see more consolidation over time.

Rick: What advice would you give to a client who's thinking about retirement?

Mark: First, you need to decide what infrastructure you need going into retirement. Do you need an office setup? Do you have a personal assistant to help you with logistics?

Have you thought about being on a board? Are you exploring a business that's a passion project? Most of us are type A personalities and it's difficult to slow down. I'm taking golf lessons with my wife. We thought about the time we spend together and the time we spend apart. The fun things we do together and the nonprofits we support we can do together. We are also working to make rums and whiskey. This was first a vanity project and it may turn into a business, but we are having fun. I joined two boards but didn't go on a third because I want to spend more time with my wife. Retirement to me is not playing golf all the time or stopping and doing nothing. That's why it's life 2.0. There are still things I want to do, including more travel. And I may decide to get into running a business like asset management, for example. Leaving yourself open to the possibilities, that's the key.

Chapter 3

The Right Culture Is Nonnegotiable

"Culture will eat strategy for lunch."

—Peter Drucker

Leaders focused on asset growth understand that creating a special workplace environment helps with recruitment, retention, and client experience. Any organization not focused on its culture will ultimately underperform. We all know that in the wealth management space human capital is the most valuable capital. A great organizational culture must serve all of the stakeholders: clients, shareholders, partners, and employees, as well as the larger communities around them. So, what makes one culture better than another? It's not membership at a gym, free food, or flexible hours. While those perks are all very nice, what I have experienced over the past 34 years and especially over the past 5 years since I've been traveling throughout North America as a consultant and speaker is that people want

31

to be valued, appreciated, and respected. They want to be recognized for their contribution and not just quietly given a pay raise.

Throughout our industry's history, we have seen what happens when an organization's culture is primarily focused on only one part of the three-legged stool: shareholders, clients, or employees. We have seen cultures that have a short-term focus of hitting sales targets miss the opportunity to do the right thing for the client. Yes, everyone likes to increase margins and increase revenue; however, if the three-legged stool is not well balanced, it will fall over eventually. We see that on the front page of the *Wall Street Journal* virtually every year. The true culture revealed in front of the world. Are you proud of your culture? If not, what will you do about it?

Great cultures have a clear vision and purpose. For example, when I hear advisors say, "We want to make a meaningful difference in people's lives," I know those may be hollow words, but it's the first step. When I hear a market leader say, "We want to create the best work environment for our people and the best environment to serve our clients," I know at the very least they are thinking about the people and what matters to them. These leaders may not get everything right, but at least they are putting their energy behind creating a place where people can feel valued and have the opportunity to grow. But ultimately actions speak the loudest. It's nice to have printed mission statements about how we take care of our people, clients, and community, but it's all about our deeds. Ultimately people vote with their feet. What do I mean by that? Clients vote with their feet if they give you assets. Advisors vote with their feet if they join your team. And of course the opposite is true, too. If clients are unhappy, they vote with their feet and walk themselves and their assets to another advisor.

Over the past five years I have worked with over 100 wealth management firms representing some of the most prestigious and most successful in the world. They all have three things in common: a desire to improve the client experience, a desire to increase asset growth organically, and a desire to attract top talent. The leaders at these firms understand that if they exceed client expectations, they will likely gain more wallet share and more introductions. A great client experience creates loyal and happy clients, which is very good for the bottom line. But here is the secret (if it can even be called a secret): a great client experience starts with a great organizational culture. You cannot have a great client experience and a poor workplace culture. If people are not happy working in the environment you have created, you will not be able to deliver a consistently positive client experience. Your job as the leader is to put a smile (metaphorically speaking) on the faces of the people on your team, advisors, and support staff, and so on. You must do this before you can put a smile on the client's face. Said differently, happy people inside a firm will make happy clients. It's that simple. Therefore, the formula for a great client experience is having the right people in the right roles with the right culture.

Of course I would not be talking about the importance of culture if it were not an issue. Based on my experiences derived from thousands of meetings with advisors, over 72 percent of advisors are not satisfied with where they work. According to *Forbes*, unhappy employees outnumber happy ones by two to one worldwide. Therefore, it should come as no surprise that thousands of advisors change firms each year. Those who move to the independent model want more control over their business; the decision to move to another firm is not always driven by compensation. These advisors want more control, the ability to create their own brand, the possibility of keeping more of what they earn, and the potential opportunity to one day sell their business.

In my time as a consultant and speaker, I have presented to thousands of advisors across North America. It is crystal clear to me the minute I walk into an office what kind of culture is present. Leaders who believe in the importance of a great culture work very hard to create a special workplace where people are happy and enjoy their work. You can feel a sense of community. It doesn't just happen; it requires a conscious decision to create the right vision and the right environment. You can recognize these types of environments immediately because when a client or guest walks into the office, they are celebrated, not merely tolerated. The first person who sees the client offers a big smile and with little effort addresses the client by name. When clients hear their name, it's music to their ears. That's what I call making an emotional deposit. The client can't help but think that these people care about them and that they are organized and focused. They are professionals.

Getting the culture right also means being relentless about hiring the right people who will fit into the culture you're building. Once you establish a great culture, the right people will see it as a major benefit. Of course, the wrong people care less about that culture, and worse, may undermine the good things going on. The wrong people are toxic to a company culture. I call these people *victims*; they enjoy complaining, are never satisfied, and are frequently negative. These are the people who will keep your firm from becoming a great place. As a leader, you might need to ask yourself if what you are creating, promoting, and allowing is negative for the culture. You need to take responsibility.

When I was a manager, I always wanted people to feel they had two families, one at home and one at the office. I had holiday parties throughout the year, not just in December. I made it my practice to include children for Halloween and Thanksgiving celebrations, encouraged community participation, and celebrated both people's personal and professional milestones. A few times a year we'd join together to support a major fundraising effort. The best managers are always seeking ways to make these types of emotional deposits. It can be as simple as sending a note to someone to recognize his performance or doing a favor for your colleague. It's not just about silently respecting people, it's about showing people you respect them. There isn't some magical secret to creating an outstanding culture; it's really about doing the simple things. Before anyone starts to focus on creating a better business strategy, it's key to get these fundamentals right.

Ask yourself:
- What does a great business culture mean to me?
- What do employees say about our office/firm to their friends and clients?
- What do clients say about my office/firm? (If you're not sure, ask them.)

- Are emails returned on a timely basis?
- Are leaders building confidence or tearing it down?
- Is transparency valued?
- Is speed valued—a sense of urgency for the client and your team?
- Are people collaborating or just talking about it?
- Are people committed or compliant?
- Does the culture inspire creativity?

I have visited more than 975 offices in the wealth management industry throughout the United States and 14 other countries. The culture of each office is apparent to me—and any other visitor—within 10 minutes of arriving. To me, a great business culture is characterized by complete transparency and trust. People in a healthy firm culture are engaged, excited, and enthusiastic— whether the client is in the room or not. A great culture is an environment in which people can speak their minds, where they can express their opinions, and where they can challenge a colleague in a professional and respectful way. I can't think of anyone who doesn't value transparency and collaboration. It's not just what you say but how you say it. Constructive conflict is not necessarily a bad thing—it's often how you come up with the best solution. This needs to start at the top of the house. As I said before, lead by example.

Unfortunately, most business cultures are still built around the expectation that everyone needs to play nice in the sandbox or suffer the consequences for professionally challenging a colleague or a superior. Businessman Charles

Koch describes the fallout of complacency in the workplace in his book, *Good Profit*:

> There's a tendency for many in successful companies to rest on their laurels and become complacent, self-protective, and less innovative. In such bureaucratic cultures, employees can survive only by running with the herd. Decline sets in.

Such cultures stifle talent and exhaust leaders. Good leaders want to make a difference, be part of a winning team, express their creativity, and excel professionally, but if the culture within which they find themselves is bureaucratic and stagnant, they might find their growth and leadership stunted. If, as a leader, you find yourself in such a culture, you have two options: change it or leave it.

Change It or Leave It

In my work, I often hear the excuse, "We have a company-wide corporate culture and I really don't have any control over what goes on locally." In many cases, ground-level leaders feel it is impossible to create a culture in the local market because they believe everyone has to march to the orders created in the home office.

I couldn't disagree more. When people work for you, regardless of whether you are a team leader or a manager at an Independent Broker Dealer (IBD), RIA, bank trust, or wirehouse, you set the tone. Your behavior and the decisions you make every day *create* the local culture. As a local leader, you can and should take responsibility for creating not only an individual team culture but also a local office culture.

Ask yourself:
- Do people trust each other in my workplace? (If they don't, how often do you talk about what values you stand for?)
- How can I change the culture to better serve all the people in the firm? (You can only do this if you have a sense of humility and you care—really care—about the people.)

Leaving a toxic culture you cannot change is not a passive act. In many ways, a key leader's departure is a way of bringing that culture to a crisis, which may lead the firm toward positive change down the line. When top talent exits, the organization suffers and talent will continue to exit until a toxic firm finally acknowledges it's in a crisis.

Transparency Transforms Cultures

Not so long ago, during a consulting engagement, I had the privilege of experiencing complete transparency within an organization. The company's CEO, Bob, was as candid with me behind closed doors as he was when we started to engage in open discussions with his partners and senior team. He had no hidden agendas, his message was consistent, and his ego was in check.

The best way a leader can demonstrate transparency is to show vulnerability and to not camouflage weaknesses (which may well be obvious to others anyway!). Bob's self-awareness and humility made it easy for the group to openly discuss issues within the organization. We were able to identify some of the firm's blind spots as well as some of the ugly spots. No organization or group of individuals can move forward until all issues are identified. The group must be able to honestly assess their own weaknesses. Such effective collaboration emerges within business cultures that sincerely encourage transparency and promote intellectual democracy—which ultimately creates a culture in which the best ideas win.

Ask your people:
- Can you describe our culture?
- Is our culture consistent with your values?
- Is our culture consistent with your actions?
- What cultures do you see in other businesses that we can learn from?
- How do people inside our organization treat one another?
- How do you show respect on a regular basis?
- Do you have an open-door policy?
- Does everyone in the organization describe the culture the same way you do?

As our business continues to become increasingly commoditized, clients will have more and more options. Therefore, creating a successful culture will be paramount to attracting and retaining clients. Clients can feel when a company has a special culture and this intangible quality makes all the difference. So, what exactly creates a positive company culture? The top-10 qualities that I most commonly see in businesses with a strong company culture are:

1. Everyone in the organization feels valued, recognized, and respected. Everyone feels relevant and that they are

    making a contribution to the big picture. This means everyone including the intern you just hired.

2. The organization celebrates diversity of people and ideas. It values overall health.

3. The organization values speed and operates with a sense of urgency. Two days to return emails or phone calls is *not* acceptable.

4. The organization's focus is on solutions versus products.

5. The organization has a clear vision and purpose. Leaders and employees can answer the following questions: Why do we exist? Where are we going, how are we getting there, and how are we different?

6. People are recognized for taking risks and trying new things. Failing is okay.

7. The organization promotes complete transparency. All employees understand why a decision is made and why a certain strategy will be implemented.

8. Celebrating milestones and making time for fun is a priority.

9. The organization promotes volunteerism and works in communities to make a difference to those who are less fortunate.

10. The organization is a meritocracy, meaning it is performance driven and client centric.

Finally, let's not make this discussion of culture more complicated than it needs to be. Do you agree that creating a great client experience is good for business and the only way to create a sustainable growth model? If so, start by spending a lot more energy on hiring the right people and making sure the people on your team are in the right roles, because over time skills may become worthless or your team may become complacent. We are in the people business; therefore, hire nice people who actually like being around people, who can do the job, and who are motivated to grow personally and professionally. Think about these key words on a daily basis: *respect, transparency, empowerment, compassion, vision, recognition*, and *results*. But more importantly, make these key tenets the foundation of your business.

Chapter 4

Leaders Collaborate Effectively

"If you have an apple and I have an apple and we exchange these apples, then you and I will still each have one apple. But if you have an idea and I have an idea and we exchange these ideas, then each of us will have two ideas."

—*George Bernard Shaw*

Growth is impossible for most organizations without effective collaboration. Leaders with a growth mindset embrace collaboration. They know what they don't know, aren't afraid to seek help, and aren't afraid to hire people smarter than they are. Of course, effective collaboration requires a strong culture that rewards and recognizes people that are strong collaborators. Without a well-thought-out process collaboration becomes much more difficult. The future will not reward the solo act as much as a well-organized team that enjoys working together to make a difference.

Creativity in creating an exceptional client experience will become even more important moving forward and collaboration will play a key role.

When I started in this business, *collaboration* was not a word that was used much. Building a business was highly transactional. We were all swimming with the sharks and each of us was rowing the boat alone. Most of us were sole practitioners; two advisors joined forces only out of necessity for succession planning.

Fast-forward to today and you read statements such as "competition makes us faster; collaboration makes us better" in virtually every business vision statement. Collaboration is the backbone of the thriving cultures we strive to develop in our businesses. In the RIA, IBD, and bank trust world, collaboration can make or kill a business. If you are in the bank trust business, then you probably already know that the best advisors are also the best collaborators. They know how to leverage the bank and its resources for the benefit of clients. They respect others and are well-liked. They get the job done. They don't allow their own egos to get in the way.

It's vital to strike the right balance between collaboration and making independent decisions because there are definitely times when collaboration can slow you down a great deal. I once worked with a CEO who runs a $2 billion RIA. He was a very smart and driven guy, but he needed to discuss every decision, even the smallest one, with the partners. This slowed down everyone, at every level, creating a vacuum that affected all aspects of the business. Sometimes decisions by committee make sense, but sometimes that extra input is not necessary. Creating the right balance and knowing the right time to collaborate is key.

Collaboration in action is demonstrated in specific situations and over time. Individuals who are labeled "collaborators" accumulate the reputation and earn the respect of an effective leader and cement that branding incrementally over an extended period of time. Leadership isn't on demand nor is it delivered only when needed; it is expected on a daily basis. And leadership, like collaboration, happens both when people are watching and when no one is watching. It is demonstrated in conversations, both one-on-one and in group settings, but most importantly it is shown by your actions. Effective leaders are aware that one leadership step backward requires at least five steps forward to recover. Authentic leaders don't proclaim themselves as the leader; rather their coworkers, peers, or clients view them as leaders.

I advanced my personal understanding of earned and respected leadership after collaborating with and observing Craig Pfeiffer when we worked together at Morgan Stanley. In his 30 years of industry experience, Craig has long advocated that demonstrating leadership generates more leadership opportunities, and ultimately management responsibility. Craig also promoted this notable theme: successful leaders require followers, and people follow leaders whom they connect with.

Connecting with people in your local business group, within the firm and across the industry, is often misrepresented as networking and navigating. Frequently, it is framed vertically in the organizational chart and horizontally with peers and colleagues. However, the secret to effective collaboration and respected leadership is connecting diagonally: "up and over" and "down and over" the organization.

Creating and sustaining diagonal relationships requires approachability, availability, and willingness to engage. This action is more critical in today's organizations with multiple (and vested) stakeholders requiring an extraordinary level of collaboration. Leaders who are accessible and participatory and contribute to the larger effort are quickly identified. They reinforce their approachability by listening, understanding, and using every interaction as an opportunity to learn. The better-informed leader is able to make better decisions and deliver a positive impact.

Approachability is crucial for the interactions and the interplay that results. Interactions are moments of both commercial and personal activity. The personal element of an interaction for a leader is the opportunity to teach, advise, and help others help themselves. These moments of personal impact help develop the talents of the followers, build their personal capabilities, enhance their confidence, and bind their followership.

Long known yet often overlooked is the importance of talent development. A leader who understands, and remembers, that "building the skills of the organization" is one of his most important priorities, then has the ability to describe a vision, set the strategies, and marshal the resources to successfully execute. Leaders are responsible for setting the goals and establishing the path, identifying the midstream milestones, and attentively enforcing accountability. When they simultaneously create a culture of optimism, persistence, and resilience they are able to achieve collective success.

Diagonal relationships and collaboration assure connectivity to other inputs, provide insight to changes unfolding, and accelerate broad-based execution. In an era with an abundance of data and metrics delivering mind-consuming measurement and analysis, it is still "about the people." When leaders engage across the organization they have followers, prepared and willing. And, remember, clients are people, too!

Collaboration Is a Competitive Advantage

Leaders who can build cultures where true collaboration exists have a competitive advantage because collaboration leverages all the strengths that exist within their teams and organizations. Collaboration must start at the top of a firm for it to be an effective component of the corporate culture. A collaborative culture enhances both morale and results, as teams are inherently more capable (and enjoyable) than are individuals. Perhaps unseen, collaboration is the power to create mutual accountability, as team members who are relied upon to achieve broadly communicated objectives are far more motivated. Finally, collaboration serves as a bulwark against negative internal conflict as the individual goals align with those of the team.

"There is more than one right answer."

—*Dewitt Jones*

Effective Collaborators:
- Check their ego at the door.
- Are able to acknowledge that two heads are better than one.

- Are bridge builders who are always looking to connect people.
- Are generous. They give help, encouragement, and other resources as needed.
- Are curious. They like asking the right questions, such as "Why?" They don't interrogate, and they follow their natural curiosity, peeling back the onion on complex issues.
- Listen to understand, not just to reply.
- Are flexible.
- Are self-motivated and inspiring.
- Are confident. They feel good about where they are going and so they welcome any and all suggestions about how to get there in a better way.
- Value all opinions. They know everyone has something to offer—and they are committed to ensuring that everyone has a chance to be heard and to contribute.
- Seek opportunities to recognize the contributions of others.

"Everyone you will ever meet knows something you don't."

—*Bill Nye*

Collaboration Requires Diversity and Respect

When collaborating, be respectful of diversity in all forms, including the diversity of ideas, cultural backgrounds, and communication and leadership styles. In a group setting, not everyone will value what you value, not everyone will like what you like, but mutual respect goes far and it starts from you. In my consulting assignments I find many leaders are challenged by diversity of thought.

Surround yourself with a formal or informal board of advisors comprised of people you can count on for honest feedback and assessment. The key to this network is diversity. If everyone in your chosen peer group thinks just like you do, then it will be a waste of your time. Surrounding yourself with people who are different from you adds an invaluable dimension to your professional growth and expands the boundaries of your thinking and creativity. I firmly believe that people who can't or choose not to expand their boundaries do so out of fear—fear that they will be challenged—and lack of confidence. Surrounding yourself with "yes" people is a waste of time and energy. Differing perspectives are your friends. Challenges that expand your worldview are paramount to personal and professional growth and being an effective leader. By being open to new perspectives, you allow yourself to consider issues in a broader light. This requires a lot of humility, which itself is a necessary quality for a strong leader. The wider your worldview lens, the better you will be able to serve your clients and your team.

"You can already get your own point of view for free."
—*Lee Iacocca*

Chapter 5

Coaching Advisors to Grow the Business

"Without a coach, people will never reach their maximum capabilities."

—*Bob Nardelli*

You Can't Coach Desire

Bill Bowerman: "Nobody can coach desire, Pre," the track coach at the University of Oregon said to Steve Prefontaine in the 1998 movie *Without Limits*, a great movie about what it takes to have heart. William Jay "Bill" Bowerman was an American track and field coach and co-founder of Nike, Inc. Over his career, he trained 31 Olympic athletes, 51 All-Americans, 12 American record-holders, 22 NCAA champions and 16 sub-four-minute milers. Leaders with a growth mindset invest in the growth of others. It's the best way to have an impact and leave a legacy. In the long run, no one will remember if you recruited three top producers or you grew your revenues by 30 percent. But people with whom you had a meaningful impact will remember you forever. That is how great leaders create more great leaders. They do this both informally, by setting an example that others want to emulate, and formally, by consciously and conscientiously investing time in developing the talents of the people they work with. But they understand that you can't coach desire. It's the biggest mistake I made as a manager in terms of coaching: trying to motivate the unmotivated. It's not the one who outright lets you know that he or she has no interest in growing or coaching or receiving help from you or anyone else. This advisor is being honest with the manager and him- or herself. It's the advisor who placates you and tells you what you want to hear who will have you spinning your wheels. That's the one who will drain your energy because it's in your nature to help people, to make a difference. It doesn't take much to get hooked into believing that these people are committed because that's what we want to believe. Therefore, before you focus on coaching be sure your advisors or managers are not only open to but committed to improving.

> "Most people, even though they don't know it, are asleep."
>
> —*Anthony DeMello, Awareness*

Many people are unaware of their potential, or most certainly the depth of their potential, until someone points it out to them. Even if they are aware of it, they may not be able to reach it without a helping hand from someone with more experience and know-how. That's where coaching comes in. Many live in an insular world and measure results

What Do You Want to Talk About Today?

The Coaching Conversation

based on poor information. For example, when someone says, "I'm doing well," I like to ask *relative to what*. Are you measuring against firm skills and objectives; are you setting your own standards? As Mark Sutton (former president of UBS) used to say, "Anyone can seem like they are running fast next to an oak tree."

A Parable: The Eagle Who Died a Chicken

A man found an eagle's egg and put it in a nest of a barnyard hen. The eaglet hatched with the brood of chicks and grew up with them. All his life the eagle did what the barnyard chicks did, thinking he was a barnyard chicken. He scratched the earth

(Continued)

(*Continued*)

for worms and insects. He clucked and cackled. And he would thrash his wings and fly a few feet into the air.

Artwork by Rick Capozzi

Years passed and the eagle grew very old. One day he saw a magnificent bird above him in the cloudless sky. It glided in graceful majesty among the powerful wind currents, with scarcely a beat on his strong golden wings. The old eagle looked up in awe.

"Who's that?" he asked.

"That's the eagle, the king of the birds," said his neighbor. "He belongs to the sky. We belong to the earth—we're chickens."

So the eagle lived and died a chicken, for that's what he thought he was.

—*Anthony DeMello*

Earn the Right to Coach

In the right environment and with the right coaching, we all have the potential to reach new heights. Great leaders know this, but too many on-the-ground managers do not. When I ask managers how many coaches they had when they were an advisor, only about 20 percent say they had coaches who made a difference in their career development. That's true for me as well. This fact is unfortunate, but perhaps not surprising. When you think about it, how much training have you had that provided you with the tools necessary to make a difference in someone else's behavior? Many people believe coaching is important, but far too many don't take the time to master the skill.

I Don't Coach Because:
- I'm too busy—47 percent
- My advisors are not receptive—24 percent
- I'm not sure how to do it—15 percent
- There's no incentive associated with the action—11 percent

Source: Spectrum Group

I encourage you as part of your own leadership and professional development to learn how to coach effectively. Like everything else it takes time and a lot of practice to become effective. The highest compliment someone can pay you is asking for your help, to be coached by someone she respects and who has achieved success. And you yourself cannot be an effective coach if you are not coached from time to time—no matter what stage of your career you are in.

When we talk about relationships, we have to understand feelings and be able to identify our own feelings and those of the people we're working with—whether it's through coaching or just plain trying to understand a team member or client. First, identify the feelings of the person with whom you are interacting so that you can determine whether he is in a negative or positive state. If the person is coming from a negative place, you can help him take action toward a more positive state. Identifying the right feelings and choosing the right words could help you have a more effective coaching conversation. The following pairs of feelings may be useful for learning how to identify different types of emotions:

Turn the negative . . .	. . . into the positive
Suspicion	Trust
Fear	Hope
Sadness	Joy
Weakness	Strength
Unfulfilled	Satisfaction
Rejection	Support
Confusion	Clarity
Shyness	Curiosity
Boredom	Involvement
Frustration	Contentment
Inferiority	Superiority
Repulsion	Attraction
Hurt	Relief
Loneliness	Community
Hate	Love
Anger	Affection
Scarcity	Abundance
Unimaginative	Creative
Insensitivity	Compassion
Insecurity	Confidence

"The day soldiers stop bringing you their problems is the day you have stopped leading them."

—*Colin Powell*

As I said earlier, I encourage you to carefully consider whom you choose to coach. Your time is precious. Focus on people who will appreciate what you have to offer and will do something with the guidance you provide. If you can't measure the progress it's difficult to make adjustments and as a result the conversation becomes just emotional.

One of the coaches I have worked with over the years as a professional is Dr. Tim Ursiny, the CEO of Advantage Coaching & Training. Tim has taught thousands of leaders coaching skills and truly understands what makes a successful coach. Tim emphasizes the importance of a coach having two sides: the soft side and the hard side. The soft side includes things like being a good listener, being inspirational, building trust quickly, asking powerful questions, and truly believing in the coachee. The hard side is the ability to challenge someone, hold him accountable, set objectives, and stretch him to his potential. The soft side alone is inadequate because it creates comfort and potential complacency. The hard side alone does not create the safety that the coachee needs to be vulnerable, admit mistakes, and show humility. Most coaches tend to be weighted more heavily on either the soft or the hard side, but the best coaches develop both sides and with it the ability to be creative and drive performance. They build a positive rather than a punitive accountability in which the coachee is recognized for her performance and challenged to perform at her highest level.

Great coaches must also differentiate from pure Socratic Method–based coaching versus mentoring. Both pure coaching and mentoring are valuable, but they offer different ways of interacting with the coachee. They can be combined for a powerful impact, but this only works if the coach knows the difference between the two styles and is able to apply whichever is needed for the situation at hand. With mentoring, the mentor is the expert. To be a mentor you often have to have a track record of coaching success or at least be able to prove your expertise on the topic. People often want mentors instead of Socratic Method–based coaches because they want to hear your advice; they want to know how you did what you did. In Socratic Method–based coaching your expertise is not necessarily part of the discussion, it's more about your ability to pull out your coachee's expertise, wisdom, and creativity and focus them on action and accountability. Thus, a coach who has never worked as a financial advisor can still coach a financial advisor.

According to Tim, the challenge is that many, if not most, managers tend to "tell" too much rather than ask powerful questions that get the coachee to self-discover the answers. If you have the discipline and the skill to get your coachees to determine answers for themselves, then you get more ownership, buy-in, and accountability from your coachees throughout the process. If they tell you what they need to do, how they need to do it, and by when they will get it done, they are much more likely to go after that outcome with ownership and passion.

It may sound easy to use questions to help people self-discover, but Tim frequently points out that the problem with that method is conditioning. In most educational experiences, we are rewarded for coming up with an answer and solving a problem. We are not rewarded as frequently for our ability to ask really good questions. When coaching, many managers feel (due to good intentions and conditioning) the strong urge to provide the answer for the coachee. While this can be helpful at times, there are other times where this approach will be harmful to the coaching process and create resistance from the coachee. Therefore, the best coaches must have the ability, through practice, to go beyond their conditioning and approach their coaching with complete awareness of when they are asking versus when they are telling.

Alternatively, when a coachee is willing, ready to act, and it is not necessary for him to become a better thinker/problem-solver on a certain topic, then it is fine to mentor. When the coachee is resistant, puts up blocks, or is unwilling or unable to figure out his solutions and actions himself, then you will want to employ more questions and reflections to get to the desired outcomes.

On the topic of resistance, Tim and I have discussed the fact that many advisors are not willing to be coached and he has shared a few insights on this issue. The first is that higher-performing advisors are actually statistically more willing to be coached than lower-performing advisors. He hypothesizes that this is due to higher-end advisors being more driven and constantly wanting to outperform others or even their own past performance.

His other insight is that, in his experience, most advisors are actually more willing to be coached than it first appears. In fact, he would go so far as to say that out of

10 people who appear unwilling to be coached, only one is truly unwilling. The key is in how you frame the coaching. The initial engagement must tap into the potential coachee's motivators, not what motivates the coach or the firm. Hard-driving, confident, fast-paced advisors tend to be motivated by results and growth. When they believe that coaching will get them better results, and, if they respect the coach, they will be much more likely to engage in coaching.

Advisors who are kind, patient, more reflective individuals may be less motivated by results or less focused on image focus, but they can be highly coachable when they see how working with a coach will create more stability and security in their lives. Individuals who are more analytical, systems-oriented, and logical are more open to coaching when they see the logic behind it, when it is presented as a clear process, and when it increases efficiencies.

It is important for a coach to uncover the personality and motivations of the coachee in the initial discovery session in order to frame the coaching appropriately. When this is done well, the number of people willing to be coached increases dramatically.

Whether the coachee is focused on results/growth, image/impact, stability/security, systems/efficiencies, or any combination of these, the key is to help the coachee achieve the outcomes she wants. Tim has told me that one of his most valuable questions in his discovery meeting is, "What does success look like?" He wants the coachee to paint a vivid picture for him of the intended outcomes from the engagement. Subsequent coaching is all done with this outcome in mind and every action step generated through the coaching should be relevant to that vision. He also likes to ask, "What will achieving that do for you?" This question helps coaches get to the root motivators. Tim also shares that if the coachee does not show some level of energy or passion when answering that question then she is likely not motivated enough to put in the hard work to go after that goal.

People often ask about when to use an inside coach (the manager) versus when to use an outside coach. Tim offered the following:

Use an inside coach when:
- It is essential for you, as the coach, to have a complete understanding of all the internal moving parts and culture (i.e., you are concerned that your lack of knowledge could lead to poor action steps for the coachee).
- The coachee respects and trusts you and feels safe enough to be honest and open.
- You want to build your reputation within your firm for your coaching skills and have the ability to get great outcomes.

Use an outside coach when:
- You have not sufficiently mastered both the soft and hard sides of being a great coach.
- The coachee will be more open and honest if the person is on the outside.
- You are too close to the individual and he may benefit more from an unbiased perspective.

The bottom line is that you should use whichever type of coach will help the coachee get the fastest and most powerful outcomes.

One of the best ways you can demonstrate value is to be the most effective coach in your market. Having a reputation that you can actually help someone grow is a big deal, because most don't have this skill set. If you're committed to making a difference in people's lives, become an outstanding coach. But like so many things in our business, one never truly masters coaching. Rather, you continuously aim to be a little more effective each time.

A 9–Step Process to Achieve Coaching Success

Before engaging in the following coaching process, it's critical to set up a discovery meeting between you and the advisor. It's an opportunity to get to know one another and understand what you're hoping to achieve through the process. It also helps determine whether you can provide the right value to the particular advisor. This meeting should not be a review of the advisor's pipeline; that can be part of the discussion, but the main focus should help determine whether the coach and advisor are best matched to engage in a coaching relationship. This process is a nonstarter if neither party is motivated by the engagement. Additionally, if the advisor says he knows it all when it comes to his business, the engagement is over before it has even begun. The advisor with a growth mindset is always looking for ways to improve, right up to his last breath.

Step 1 in the process is to start with a belief audit to get a clear understanding of the advisor's worldview and beliefs. First, does she believe in coaching? How does she feel about teams? Understanding potential blocks to the process sets the stage. I can't begin to tell you how much time I have wasted trying to change people. It's exhausting. People change when they have a clear purpose and are motivated to change. You are not a magician. And generally people are most open to changing behavior when they are feeling pain.

Step 2 focuses on time management. Ask the advisor the following questions: How do you spend your time? How do you define high payoff activities? How do you manage an increase in capacity? How do you leverage resources? With technology brain hacking you at every turn, you need to help the advisor stay focused on what really matters. Help him identify all the noise in his life. There are 525,600 minutes in a year: help the advisor align his intentions with his actions.

Step 3 involves conducting a gap analysis. Hone in on helping the advisor answer the following questions: What are your strengths? What are the gaps that impede you from delivering on your promises? We all have blind spots, by the way. Help him identify his gaps. During this step you also want to analyze his level of emotional intelligence and self-awareness. Determine what area of his work would be best served by developing new skills. Is it capital markets they need help with, planning, team collaboration? And so on.

Step 4 establishes an individual's value proposition. Ask: Who are you? Why do you do what you do? What makes you different from others in the business? Whom do you do business with? Help him become very clear on the idea that the advisor is the solution and clients ultimately buy him versus a product or service. Help the advisor discover, articulate, and deliver a confident value proposition.

Step 5 involves business development. What are the best asset-gathering opportunities for the advisor? What are her talents and passions? There is little point in trying to convince someone to engage in an activity in which she doesn't have either the skill set or right mindset. For example, if you choose a form of exercise that you actually enjoy, you're much more likely to stick with it. But if you don't enjoy the activity, your enthusiasm will likely fade very quickly. Be mindful of helping advisors develop the right talents.

Step 6 focuses on establishing a clear set of service tiers. Basically, this step involves creating three service models in order to create unparalleled service for each client. Help the advisor identify his client segments and assess the level of service he is providing to each client segment. Help him tighten up his service model.

Step 7 analyzes the client meetings, including discovery, quarterly reviews, client events, and so forth. How effective and efficient are these meetings? How is the closing process? Who participates in these meetings? How does the advisor determine effectiveness when it comes to her own communication? Where does she get feedback on her communication style?

Step 8 focuses on client feedback. Help the advisor create the proper action plan to engage in a systematic process of receiving feedback from clients. Help the advisor decide if a client board of advisors would be appropriate.

Step 9 includes work/life balance. As the coach and/or manager are you truly interested in the overall well-being of the advisor? Or are you only focused on the metrics? Genuinely being concerned about the person you are coaching will make you stand out as a coach because that's not the norm. As a coach and/or manager, you may play many roles—one might be the therapist while another might be the cheerleader. Help the advisor achieve an appropriate work/life balance. An advisor who is physically fit and mentally capable is more likely to achieve the growth mindset needed to excel in his business.

Once again, you have to earn the right to coach someone. Just because you have a title doesn't translate into the right to coach. Read, practice, be coached, and ask for feedback. After 10,000 hours at any discipline we can say we know something.

Chapter 6

Credibility Is the Foundation

"Watch your thoughts, they become words;
Watch your words, they become actions;
Watch your actions, they become habits;
Watch your habits, they become character;
Watch your character, for it becomes your destiny."

—*Lao Tzu*

A growth mindset is rooted in credibility. Great leaders are credible and work hard to stay credible. Credibility is how leaders gain the confidence, trust, hearts, and minds of all the stakeholders—clients, advisors, partners, and colleagues. Credibility is the foundation of leadership, no matter how large or small your team. If people don't believe in the messenger, they won't believe in the message—it's that simple. Credible people under-promise and over-deliver. My friend, John Decker, a manager at UBS, wrote a terrific book titled *Success Is Not a Secret*. When talking about recruiting and retention, John clearly stands out. He writes in his book that "trust is the most important factor in retention. More than anything, trust comes from being truthful. Telling the truth is not always fun, but it's always the right thing to do. Any circumstance can be used to build trust. Even when an advisor asks for something you can't give them, or behaves inappropriately and must be corrected, it is an opportunity to build trust. By being combative, you'll lose them. By being honest, straightforward, and consistent, you'll continue to build that trust." I have known John for a long time, and he is not afraid to say no and he is fair and consistent.

Elements of trust:
1. Trust is a function of doing what you said you would do.
2. Credibility is demonstrated by your ability to ask compelling and thought-provoking questions.
3. We trust people who respect our point of view and values.
4. We trust people who are competent.
5. We trust people who have a strong conviction of their recommendations.
6. We trust people who can empathize.
7. Credible people focus more on deeds than words.
8. Credible leaders are fully transparent at all times.
9. Those with a growth mindset look for opportunities to lead from the front.

Consider this:
- Leadership is personal. It's about you, not the brand or your firm.

Leadership is about:
- What you believe in

- Your worldview
- Your values
- Your principles
- Your character

Simply, leadership is about your credibility. And the best way to gain credibility is to under-promise and over-deliver.

> "We conclude from our interviews and case analyses that credibility, respect and loyalty are earned primarily when leaders demonstrate by their actions that they believe in the inherent self-worth of others."
> —*James M. Kouzes and Barry Z. Posner, Credibility: How Leaders Gain It and Lose It, Why People Demand It*

Credible leaders put the client before profits and people ahead of politics or self-interest. We know that the financial markets and the workplace environment will continue to be volatile, and uncertainty is something we as leaders need to turn to our advantage. We can use uncertainty to create a competitive edge for ourselves, and we need credibility to lead our people through uncertain times.

Credibility Must Be Earned

Great leaders don't take their credibility for granted: they earn it, cultivate it, and nurture it. Competence and trust are the foundation of credibility. Being completely transparent with both your team and your clients will also help you establish credibility.

In their book, *Credibility: How Leaders Gain It and Lose It, Why People Demand It,* James Kouzes and Barry Posner identify the six disciplines of credibility as:

1. Discovering yourself
2. Appreciating constituents
3. Affirming shared values
4. Developing capacity
5. Serving a purpose
6. Sustaining hope

We know that leadership is a contact sport—leadership is always a relationship between leaders and their teams. Since strong relationships are built on understanding, leadership demands a dialogue, not a monologue. Dialogue only occurs when leaders get out of their offices and "ivory tower" equivalents and genuinely interact with the people they lead. When leaders are accessible, they are actively creating an environment in which it is safe for people to discuss whatever is on their minds.

I believe that I overcame many of my shortfalls as a young leader through significant and persistent interaction with people, through which I was able to communicate to them that I always had their best interests at heart. My actions not my words helped me become more and more credible over time. People will also be more forgiving when you make a mistake and you quickly admit it, if you're credible to begin with.

Consider this:

- Get out of your office! Practice management by walking around.

- Management by wandering around is practiced by such great leaders as Lee Iacocca and was enshrined in Tom Peters and Bob Waterman's first book, *In Search of Excellence*. It works.

Diversity

Credible leaders honor the diversity of their partners, teams, and clients. They find common ground on which everyone can build. They bring people together; they are bridge builders and they enjoy uniting people. They build a strong sense of community that fosters collaboration and trust.

Hope

Credible people are optimistic and foster hope in those around them. They talk of the future in a way that is upbeat, energetic, and inspirational. When things get difficult, they make themselves available to support the situation and do whatever it takes to make it better. They communicate often and they never stop talking about what the future will look and feel like.

Humanity and Humility

Credibility does not equal infallibility. It's important to be human with the people you lead; in fact, they will appreciate it. You are not Mr. or Mrs. Google—you are not expected to know everything. Credible people are also humble people. Humility attracts people and fosters trust (and thus credibility!). Humility creates a clearing for your own growth and creates space for others to relate to you. If you are quick to judge, people are less likely to bring you a challenge or seek advice. Help people self-discover the best answer that will serve their needs.

Honesty

Finally, credible people tell the truth even when the truth is difficult. They keep their word, and if and when circumstances change, they let others know as soon as possible. They are never spin doctors. When I was a regional director for one of the Big Four wealth management firms in the country, I reported to a CEO who loved to spend days crafting a story to explain new compensation plans for the advisors (modifying compensation plans seemed to be an annual occurrence). He believed that we should find a way to explain the new compensation to make it seem attractive. Typically, a new compensation plan was simply a pay cut. Everyone always knew it. The end result of his exercise was losing credibility with his team. You simply can't lie, or tell 90 percent of the truth, because people will know you're leaving out a piece of the puzzle. Again, never underestimate the advisor or client. Tell it like it is; it's clean and it's refreshing. With honesty comes the ability to say, "I don't know." If you don't know the answer, say so. People can tell when someone makes up an answer.

In the past, wealth management was about selling complexity or having access to products that others with less net worth didn't have. Today, it is about full transparency and simplicity. Your team, peers, and clients demand transparency. Employees want to know how and why decisions are made. They can handle the truth. Clients want to get into the weeds about cost, including how people are compensated. Tell them. They can handle the truth.

Consider this:
- If you don't know the answer, admit it by saying "I don't know."
- Tell it like it is, without trying to create something that sounds good but isn't the full truth.
- Trust your team, colleagues, and clients to be able to handle the truth.
- Keep your commitments.
- Under-promise and over-deliver.
- Ask yourself this question: How good is my word?

When I think of a manager who had instant credibility among his peers, superiors, and clients, Bill comes to mind. He was a person of few words. When dealing with the issues the company faced, he never made it about himself—he always made it about the stakeholders. While working with Bill at UBS, he never called to check on or critique my performance; he could see if my $5 billion in assets was plus or minus for the month. He saved any discussion of my performance for our quarterly reviews. When he did call, he focused on me and my personal and professional needs and challenges. After listening to me, no matter the issues, Bill always offered to help. Bill was a master of interpersonal skills. More than his personal skills, Bill's ability to challenge the status quo, to question, and to push back if something didn't make sense or could be done better is what made him credible. He was not living in a world of self-preservation; he was using himself to improve the client conditions and people on his team. He was always quick to stand up and admit his mistakes and in any situation he unfailingly did what was right. I see a pattern with credible people: they are not talkers. They are people of action and they do what they say. They don't dig in their heels when someone disagrees. Confidence seems to jump out and hit whomever they're talking to right between the eyes. They also despise bullies. They are the first to stand up for the person that needs a voice or a helping hand.

With clients, the same rule applies. If you don't agree with the client or the client is dominating the conversation or the relationship, your value is diminished. Having competency and confidence allows you to be your true self. Being the authentic you and being vulnerable makes you more credible than hiding behind one mask after another. Not allowing the other person to see who you really are leaves them questioning whether they can trust you. Never underestimate someone you're speaking to or working with, thinking they can't see through you. At the end, the essence of who you are will eventually reveal itself.

Lisa Carnoy is the U.S. Trust Division Executive for the Northeast. She also serves as Bank of America's market president for New York City. Prior to joining U.S. Trust, Lisa served as head of Global Capital Markets for Bank of America Merrill Lynch. Lisa graduated from Columbia and went on to Harvard Business School.

What immediately struck me about Lisa was her energy, confidence, and transparency. It doesn't take long to see that she has a growth mindset. I sat down with Lisa in the executive dining room at the U.S. Trust office in New York City.

Rick: Lisa, you have been successful in running several businesses; what's been your secret?

Lisa: Thank you, Rick. Whether leading Global Capital Markets or a Private Banking Division, I exude a passion for the business, belief in the team, and optimism in the long term. I don't know that it is a "secret" but it has allowed me to attract and retain some tremendously talented, committed, and decent people.

Rick: What advice would you give a manager who's running a wealth management business?

Lisa: Listen, roll up your sleeves to remove obstacles, share best practices, and say "thank you." Thank you to advisors, partners across investments, credit, risk, and especially clients and prospects. I like to go on calls with our teams and get to know our clients and prospects. I always learn from our teams—and I hope they learn from me. What questions I ask, how I probe where a client has a need, how I position our team and capabilities and so on. Also, how I follow up/create urgency around opportunities.

Rick: Everyone is talking about disruption and fee compression. What role do you think technology will play in disrupting the traditional wealth management model?

Lisa: Technology is already a massive disruptor. The key is to use it to help clients—whether ease of execution, greater transparency, broader choices, real-time data, or analytics, and so on.

Rick: Lisa, I know how much you enjoy meeting with clients or prospects. What do you believe they care most about in choosing a wealth management team?

Lisa: Clients and prospects are looking for many different things. Often, a prospect will tell me they care about a team's experience as well as chemistry. Is the advisor a good listener? Does she or he convey competence? Will they deliver a great team—and curate the entire firm? In many cases, a prospect wants to make sure that the advisor is a good fit with their spouse or children. In some situations, a specific expertise matters—perhaps wealth planning ahead of a liquidity event for a business owner or structure credit expertise or philanthropic advice.

Rick: As you know, the word *transparency* is tossed around in every organization, large or small. Transparency seems to come naturally to you. Can you explain why transparency is so important? What does it do for the culture?

Lisa: Transparency is critically important to our clients and our teams. It ranges from sharing details with a prospect or client on developing a tailored investment policy statement to what we expect going forward in terms of day-to-day coverage—to how we charge for our services—and how we will work to achieve long-term goals. As a fiduciary, transparency is core to the culture of U.S. Trust. In adhering to the fiduciary standard, our commitment first and foremost is to serve your best interests and goals and place them ahead of our own.

Chapter 7

Emotional Intelligence

"If you are tuned out of your own emotions, you will be poor at reading them in other people."

—*Daniel Goleman*

Who are you? No, don't give me your job title. If I take away your job title, your house, and your car, who are you? What is important to you? Do you know yourself? Are you aware of how you make others feel when you walk into a room? When things don't go your way, are you aware of how you react and how it affects others? *Emotional intelligence* (EI) is recognizing, understanding, and managing our own emotions.

"The unexamined life is not worth living."

—*Socrates*

Most of us are familiar with the concept of self-awareness and emotional intelligence. It's been around a long time;

in fact, the term first appeared in a 1964 paper by Michael Beldoch and gained popularity in the 1995 book, *Emotional Intelligence*, written by the author, psychologist, and science journalist Daniel Goleman. Unfortunately, being familiar with emotional intelligence does not always translate into possessing it. Becoming self-aware and staying self-aware requires tools that many leaders do not possess. It is a tragedy because great leadership begins with knowing yourself.

Leaders with a growth mindset cultivate self-awareness and have high emotional intelligence. They have empathy that allows them to make a deeper emotional connection with the client. They are not robotic. They have a process but they are flexible because they know it's first about winning the heart and then the mind. In other words, we are emotional beings. Therefore, an emotional connection needs to come first, followed by logic. In my interviews with leaders and advisors over the past 25 years, I often ask what's more important, the soft skills or the hard skills. Virtually everyone responds that the soft skills are much more important.

You may be thinking, can I really improve emotional intelligence? Although I'm not an expert, based on what I have read and my own experiences, I absolutely believe you can. I have coached a number of advisors by just pointing out a few things. For example, in response to a client who had an objection about an investment decision, one advisor would start to get defensive, his body language would change, and he would speak louder. He was not aware of how his behavior affected others. It takes focus and dedication to learn how your words and actions might be received by others. But, more importantly, you often need someone else to help you identify such issues and use them as opportunities to improve. Unfortunately, people go through life never knowing that making some minor tweaks to how they react in various situations would make a big difference in their career or personal life. Some people are simply sleepwalking.

> "Most leaders have grown familiar with the concept of self-awareness. They understand that they need to solicit feedback and recognize how others see them. But when it comes to . . . our assessments of ourselves . . . [we] can still be woefully inaccurate."
> —Erika Andersen, "Managing Yourself: Learning to Learn,"
> Harvard Business Review (March 2016)

So how do you get to know yourself? There are hundreds of books, and just as many self-awareness gurus, promising to sell you self-awareness for the modest price of admission—or the price of a meditation retreat.

In my work with thousands of leaders and wealth management professionals, I have found that it is the people with a high level of emotional intelligence who can evaluate themselves most accurately. They ask themselves "What do I think?" and more importantly, "Why do I think that?" Asking yourself these questions should help you make better decisions, have better relationships with people, and stay true to the person you hope to be. Aligning your intentions with your actions becomes a considerably smoother process once you become clear on who you are. Without a good sense of self-awareness, you can't improve in the areas you should improve.

Ask yourself:
- Who am I?
- What do I believe in? What is my philosophy?
- What do I stand for? What is my credo?
- What are my values? What are my principles?
- What frustrates me?
- What angers me?

Notably, leaders who are self-aware and spend a lot of time reflecting on what's inside their heads are much better at considering the opinions and inputs of other people. Self-aware leaders accept that their perspective may be biased or flawed and they seek to achieve greater objectivity. That attitude leaves them much more open to hearing and considering the opinions of others.

I once had a consulting engagement with a large RIA where our objective was to move the firm from no growth to an acceptable growth rate of 10 to 15 percent. Assets under management had been the same for the past three years. In this case, the members of the executive team were all very experienced, each with 30 to 40 years in the wealth management industry. After many hours of one-on-one meetings with all the partners, I concluded that the RIA was a great service organization and not a sales/marketing and service organization.

The CEO recognized the firm needed outside help and quickly implemented my suggestions. In fact, I gave them 20 action items and they moved on 17 of them within a week. Everyone was motivated. At first the CEO was not fully self-aware of his own strengths and weaknesses.

He didn't realize that he was not a sales leader and that he didn't exactly know how to identify great sales leaders. However, he did have other valuable skills that helped him succeed in his organization over the years. This self-knowledge and humility to put one's ego aside to help the greater good is the leadership difference between a firm achieving growth and one that's stagnating. But you, in your leadership role, don't need to wait until the pain is unbearable. If you're constantly reevaluating and assessing and growing as a person, you're more likely to identify the changes you need to make before they become a crisis.

Ask yourself:
- Do I listen to that inner voice about ways to improve myself?
- How well do I listen to other people that I respect?
- How do I react to views and opinions that are contrary to my own?
- Do I only listen to people who affirm my views and dismiss everything else?
- How well can I read someone? Is it obvious (or not so obvious) what they are feeling?
- What's the tone and rhythm of my voice and body language? (Video yourself in your next meeting or presentation. You don't need fancy equipment—your smartphone will do an adequate job. You will probably be surprised about how much you will learn about yourself.)
- How often am I asking for feedback regarding ways I can improve?

- Do I become overly emotional?
- How well can I put myself in other people's shoes? How well do I empathize? Do I feel what they feel— loss, joy, gratitude, regret, fear, love?

> "What are my strengths? Most people think they know what they are good at. They are usually wrong. More often, people know what they are not good at and even then people are more wrong than right. And yet, a person can perform only from strength. One cannot build performance on weakness, let alone on something one cannot do at all. We need to know our strengths in order to know where we belong. And the only way to discover your strengths is through feedback analysis."
>
> —Peter Drucker, *Managing Oneself*

With a little effort you can improve your relationships with your team, clients, family, and friends. With a lot of effort you can dramatically improve every interaction with prospects and clients. When your antenna is on high alert you become an intuitive listener who is able to really see what that person is feeling, reading between the lines and picking up on what's not being said. With high emotional intelligence you're able to properly respond to the world around you and you become a sponge in the way people connect with you on a deeper level. EI will give you the competitive edge if you stay focused on always improving.

Chapter 8

Managing Yourself and Taking Responsibility

"The way we spend our days is the way we spend our lives."

—*Annie Dillard*

Self-Care Creates Energy

If you can't manage yourself well, how can you objectively manage others and clients? And managing yourself starts with self-care. Great leaders take care of themselves and, thus, they build their careers and their lives on solid foundations. They pay attention to small, everyday things. In my experience, living a healthy lifestyle is a prerequisite to being an effective advisor and leader. Having balance is key. The successful leaders featured in this book follow

83

a daily regime of eating well, exercising regularly, getting enough sleep, and practicing mindfulness and some form of meditation. They know these everyday self-care activities are essential to managing stress, depression, and anxiety and enhancing positive energy, productivity, and concentration. Taking care of yourself means also knowing who you are. One of my favorite self-care books is *The Brain Warrior's Way* by Daniel G. Amen, MD, and Tana Amen, BSN, RN. It focuses on the interrelationships of energy, focus, moods, memory, weight, relationships, work, and overall health. So many of us are our own worst enemy. We get in the way of ourselves and we get stuck at times and cannot see the light right in front of us. Ralph Waldo Emerson said it well: "Most of the shadows of this life are caused by our standing in our own sunshine." Positive everyday habits in your personal life help you foster positive habits in your professional life and will help you grow as a leader. Great leaders know this to be true.

Bringing your "A game" starts by showing up on time and being well prepared. This might seem basic but I see people missing important meetings and opportunities because they didn't feel well or weren't fully prepared.

Breaking Through

If you are surprised by this fact, it's because you are not one of these people. In my estimation, over 50 percent of the people in the business miss the opportunity to execute on the fundamentals of their work just because they don't have the energy to do what is necessary on any given day. If you are not in the right state of mind, you're not going to ask for that introduction because you just don't feel you have that right energy, or the confidence if you get rejected. You tend to procrastinate more often than those who diligently follow good self-care practices.

Since I travel a great deal, my foremost thoughts are about guarding my health. If I catch a cold or condition that prevents me from showing up and performing my responsibilities, it doesn't matter how good I may be. I'm not present. Thus, not showing up becomes my personal brand, and I may become known as someone who's not reliable. That's why in over 1200 presentations that I delivered all over the world I have never missed one or ever been late.

Ask yourself:
- Am I satisfied with my health?
- Am I getting enough sleep?
- Do I eat a well-balanced diet?
- Do I make time for exercise?
- Do I make time for a mindfulness, religious, or spiritual practice?

If your answer to any of these questions is, "No," ask yourself:

- Why not?
- Why do I not value my health?

Leaders practicing self-care value not just their physical health, but also their emotional health. They take steps to reduce their anxiety and tension. It's difficult to perform at the top of your game professionally when you are off-balance emotionally. Being tense inhibits your ability to notice the unexpected and reduces your opportunities to be a good listener. Being emotionally balanced will open up a world of possibilities and opportunities. Writing or talking about this is the easy part; the hard part is doing it because we all know that our circumstances can change in a second—family issues, health issues, and the daily challenges of taking care of our clients. Resilience and a healthy network of friends is the best way to stay on track and keep moving forward. In short, the secret is a few meaningful, loving, and trusting relationships and making good decisions about your health. You may need to change your relationship with food, people, time and beliefs. Again, it all starts with purpose. The motivation, the staying power.

Ask yourself:
- Am I emotionally well-balanced?
- Do I spend most of my energy thinking about the past or future rather than focusing on the present?
- Do I hang onto regrets?
- What things contribute to my level of anxiety in my personal and professional life?
- How do the people in my life affect how I feel? How about the things I read or watch?
- What is my relationship with time? How do I prioritize and avoid procrastination?
- What are three specific things I can do to reduce stress and anxiety in my life?

Now take action!

"Keep close to nature's heart . . . and break clean away once in a while, and climb a mountain or spend a week in the woods. Wash your spirit clean."

—*John Muir*

Energy is something that I pay more and more attention to as I get older. I'm always on the lookout for activities or experiences that give me good energy. For me, reading biographies or books on philosophy and being around positive and authentic people gives me energy. All aspects of Nature move me. I'm very fortunate to live on a beautiful five-acre property where I can get my hands dirty by planting a tree or chopping wood or simply walk around paying attention to Nature. This experience is perfect and magical for me. Fall in love with Nature; it will always be there for you. Bask in the wonders it has to offer. To me, Nature is pure, it's truth, it's energy, it's growth, and it's life.

If your energy is not where you would like it to be, pay attention to the people in your life, what you read and watch, and your habits and lifestyle. Find what energizes you and cultivate it. Life is a marathon, not a sprint, so plan accordingly. Remember, you have the power of choice. If you want to be positive and happy, you need to make that a choice now. Don't base it on conditions (once X happens, then I'll do Y). Your attitude will affect your business. If you fall for the trap of the "more" game, you will likely live a life of constant anxiety, which will affect your "long" game. The answer is balance, discipline, gratitude, joy, and love. Your choice.

Take Responsibility

"Success on any major scale requires you to accept responsibility. . . . In the final analysis, the one quality that all successful people have is the ability to take on responsibility."

—*Michael Korda*

Ultimately, having the right energy is about taking responsibility for yourself, your decisions, and your destiny. At all stages of any career, lessons are often learned the hard way. Leaders, even the most admired ones, aren't flawless. More often than not, leaders who own their mistakes and failures and learn from these experiences are the ones who are most admired. Leaders are not victims; they don't make excuses. Leaders with a growth mindset take responsibility for their past, present, and future.

"Ninety-nine percent of all failures come from people who have a habit of making excuses."

—*George Washington Carver*

Wishful thinking does not move you forward. The only way you can control your destiny is by taking full responsibility for it. When you take full responsibility, you must deal with what is in front of you. In other words, you must accept the truth of your reality.

Let's say you have a boss, advisor, or partner with whom, for some reason, you don't get along. Things just get worse over the years, but you keep wishing he would change or treat you differently. The relationship is less than ideal. Face the reality and make your decisions based on that reality. If someone on your team is not living a healthy lifestyle and it's affecting the business, take some of the initiative and do something about it. You may have two clients who are a poor fit to your business model. Perhaps they constantly question your value, or are always complaining. Take responsibility for the situation and make a decision to do something about it.

> "I am the product of my decisions, not my circumstances."
>
> —*Stephen Covey*

Consider this when faced with a difficult situation:
- Acknowledge the situation: "I don't get along with my partner."
- Take responsibility for the situation: "Is there anything I can do to change the relationship?"
- Identify possible actions: "I will be more assertive about my boundaries and expectations. I will talk with her honestly and respectfully about our issues and see if we can figure out a way to make it better."
- Do it.

> "I have not failed. I've just found 10,000 ways that won't work."
>
> —*Thomas A. Edison*

By initiating the conversation, you are taking responsibility for the situation and taking leadership in finding a solution. You may fail, but that's okay. As a leader, you take responsibility for the failure. You carefully consider the lessons you learned from the experience. You will use these lessons to move forward. The cornerstone of a growth mindset starts with taking responsibility, because you create, promote, or allow what goes on in your environment. The first time I heard that idea was while I was attending an executive leadership course at the University of Virginia Darden School of Business. Professor Weber shared it with the attendees and it didn't quite hit me until I got back to the office.

When I was running a region, one of the managers in my region in New England had a pattern of treating people with disrespect. At the time, I would say to myself, "I didn't create this manager since I didn't hire him nor do I tolerate this form of behavior from him or anyone else." However, by keeping him on board, I allowed this pattern of behavior to persist. That was absolutely my responsibility. Taking full responsibility is not only about seeing right from wrong but also acting to do the right thing. If you or someone in your operation or home office makes a mistake, you should quickly take full responsibility no matter what. Even if the client is unlikely to learn of the error, you must always be transparent with him. The client is doing business with you—don't try to deflect the blame on the asset manager or your assistant or junior partner. Own it right away.

Ask yourself:
- What negative patterns am I creating or allowing in my life or business that aren't good for me and the people I care about?
- What am I creating that's positive?
- What am I promoting that's positive or negative to everyone around me?

That self-awareness we discussed earlier in the book is very useful in helping you to honestly answer these questions.

That last question—what are you promoting, creating and allowing. Allowing is the one most people don't acknowledge responsibility for. So, what are you allowing that's not good for the long-term success of you and your clients and everything that you care about? I'll give you a few examples to get you started.

- Do you allow your team to disrespect each other and as a result they don't work well together?
- Do you allow one person to control or manipulate you?
- Do you allow the person to whom you report to treat you unfairly or disrespectfully?
- Do you condone a team member who is not fully prepared or not knowledgeable on a topic she is expected to understand?
- Do you allow yourself to become complacent?
- Do you allow a few people in your office to create an unpleasant environment for everyone?
- Are you allowing one person to hijack a meeting?

"The price of greatness is responsibility."

—*Winston Churchill*

At the end, if you can't lead yourself successfully you certainly can't lead others effectively.

Leader/Cause	Victim/Effect
• Takes Responsibility	Blames
• Proactive	Reactive
• Decisive	Procrastinates
• Doer	Talker
• Choice	No Choice
• Possibilities	Limitations
• Powerful	Powerless
• In Control of own emotional state	Responds to other's emotional state
• Initiative	Excuses
• Optimist	Pessimist
• I'm Committed	I'll Try
• Now	Someday

The only thing that stands between a man and what he wants from life is often merely the will to try it and the faith to believe that it is possible.

—*David Viscott*

Chapter 9

Recruiting and Retaining Top Talent

"The secret of my success is that we have gone to exceptional lengths to hire the best people in the world."

—*Steve Jobs*

Leaders with a growth mindset recognize the need to recruit, develop, and deploy the talent of others. Such leaders are hyper-focused on attracting and retaining top talent. They don't just look for advisors with a big book of business. They look for talent that will grow with the firm and add good energy while doing so. The best place to start looking for leads is right in your own office. These are the people you know and who know you. You should always be looking for new advisors. That's the only way to have a sense of control over your own destiny and to ensure that you are not being held hostage by those who are a poor cultural fit.

Over the past 10 years I have asked managers in every channel what percentage of their advisors they would replace if they could wave a magic wand. Their answers run a range from 10 to 30 percent. No matter how you look at it, that's a lot of advisors. One of the ways I interpret those percentages is like this: those teams, departments, and firms are 10 to 30 percent less efficient and successful than they can be. My point is that you have room to build the type of culture that you envision; you just need to attract those advisors who will better serve the client and your overall strategy.

When I was a manager, I offered my team members an incentive of 2 percent of their trailing 12-month production for anyone who made a successful introduction and was helpful with the recruitment process. Relying on your own team to help with the recruitment process can be just as important as recruiting new talent. If your existing team is not happy, however, they will not actively promote the opportunities to others. In fact, if they themselves are unsatisfied, you might be faced with retention issues. I have also recruited advisors simply by picking up the phone and introducing myself. And, in a large market this strategy could keep you busy for a long time. Utilizing an outside recruiter is also an effective strategy. I have always had a good experience working with professional recruiters. But before I engage recruiters, I build a relationship with them. I want them to know our story so they understand who would be the right fit.

Recruiting has to start with a bold vision of where you see your office, market, or firm, be it in one, five, or ten years. You need to make a declaration, a powerful statement. A longtime friend from UBS is the best example of what's possible when you create the right culture. John Decker and I were managers at UBS for many years and I consider him one of the best recruiters of all time. What's his secret? He is very competitive and likes to win. He also never becomes complacent. As CEO Andy Grove said, "Success breeds complacency. Complacency breeds failure. Only the paranoid survive." The other secret to John's success is his ability to surround himself with talented people. He would be the first to tell you that you can't build a business without the help and cooperation of many. Finally, one of John's greatest passions is to inspire and motivate others to reach their full potential. When I first became a manager in 1990, John told me something I never forgot, and it has served me well over the years. He said, "Rick, learn to love recruiting." John's competitiveness, his emphasis on working with the most talented people, and his drive to inspire and motivate is what makes him a top recruiter. And, as I said before, paying attention to details matters. John doesn't wing anything that's important to him. To be an effective recruiting machine you need to have a process and be organized.

The recruitment process starts with creating a deep talent pipeline and never letting it run dry. When you meet with a potential new advisor, it's just like a client discovery meeting. Once you feel the advisor may be the right fit, it's time to find out everything about him (all within appropriate human resource practices, of course). As to family, where is he with kids? Are the kids out of the house? Are they in college? Is he taking care of his parents or in-laws? What's his passion? How does he spend his free time? I like to ask advisors, if money were no object, what would they be doing? During the conversation, I look to make a connection with something we both may be passionate about. Relationships are shared experiences after all. If you have an innate curiosity, you may learn something. Finally, I want to know what gets them out of bed every day. What are they hoping to achieve and what are their long-term goals? Some advisors have a very clear picture what this future looks like. For others, it's a little foggy because they have never taken the time to think and plan ahead. This is a good opportunity to help them talk about their business, their goals, and the resources needed to achieve them. When all is said and done, I want to win them over, but not by over-promising and under-delivering. If I have one secret to being successful at attracting talent, it's the following: have a solid reputation. What does your brand say about you? You must have the tenacity to make recruiting a daily activity, and you must also surround yourself with competent people who can make the onboarding process seamless for both the advisor and the clients.

During all the recruitment and deals that I have structured over the past 25 years, one thing remains certain. Without two motivated people at the table, the deal doesn't get done. I have learned that motivation is different for each person. It's not always about money. Advisors move for different reasons, but generally there is a push and pull. I have been on both sides of negotiating a deal and I find that the better you understand your market, value, and competition, the better position you are in to negotiate. In other words, do your homework. If the advisor only wants to talk about money or the deal, this is a red flag for me. I'm not interested in attracting people who are only focused on the deal. The best advisors focus on three things when they contemplate a move. The first is serving clients well. They care about taking care of their clients before anything else. The second thing is whether the culture is right for them and their team. They are concerned with the questions: Will we be happy here? Is the management team committed to excellence? And the third thing the best advisors think about is the overall compensation.

Trying to attract top advisors is an art. The advisor is trying to get 100 percent of what he or she wants and we know most of the time it's not possible. Therefore, help advisors prioritize what's most important to them. How flexible are they? Helping them be clear about their top priorities is the foundation not only to negotiating but to determining if it's the right fit for both of you. Negotiating is a highly emotional process and some advisors deal with it better than others. It's your job to help them discover what's truly important to them and to sit on the same side of the table with them. Building trust, therefore, is the number one priority when recruiting and negotiating. During this process nothing kills trust faster than breaking your promise or commitments. I consider a broken commitment as simple as being late for an appointment or promising to mail something and forgetting to do so. Again, most people are not disciplined and organized enough to keep their commitments. Therefore, if you want to stand out, pay attention to the details, follow through, and keep your word.

The biggest turnoff for the hiring manager or the advisor is rigidity. No one wants to deal with Dr. No, the person who has no flexibility and is stubborn. That's not to say that saying no doesn't ever happen or is inappropriate (be just as cautious of the person who only says yes). If the answer is "no," how are you saying it? Again, your emotional intelligence goes a long way in these situations. I once worked with a compliance manager who loved to say no. She just enjoyed the reaction, and she liked that power. I never like saying no because I tend to be a people pleaser. Therefore, if I must say no, I try to show a great deal of empathy.

One mistake I see in recruiting is making comparisons between your firm and another. Often people mistakenly compare apples to oranges. Whether you're working at an independent firm, wirehouse, bank trust, or RIA, every firm within each channel is different. Advisors sometimes make assumptions based on channel alone about what your firm offers in terms of technology, platform, support, culture, total compensation, and payout. It's vital that you are honest about everything. Make sure the details are spelled out clearly and correctly so there are no surprises down the road.

Hiring Does Not Equal Recruiting

Recruiting and hiring are two different skills. If hiring is like driving a car, recruiting is like racing in a Formula One car. To put it another way, when you're hiring, you're the buyer. When you're recruiting, you're the seller. Recruiting top talent takes a lot of skill and hard work. These people often have a large book of business as well as many options and they know it.

Consider this:
- Look at the quality of the book and the character of the person.

- Look at the last three years' track record of net new assets. Is the business growing?
- Look for people who genuinely like people: never forget we are in the relationship business. Once again, culture matters.
- Look for nice people. It's an inherent quality and it's as critical in our relationship business as any hard skill, perhaps more so because it cannot be taught. "Nice" to me means putting clients' interests first and treating everyone with respect.
- Take the Thanksgiving test. Would you ask this person over for Thanksgiving?

Just as important as what you do want out of the recruiting process is what you don't want. Do not recruit a book—recruit the person. I promise this does not reduce your recruiting success. I'm just thinking of my mistakes of recruiting the wrong people and what I've learned along the way about the best tactics to recruit the right people. Who joins your team affects retention and your environment. Do not hire people who would rather sit in front of a computer screen all day than network with people. The future will place more value on soft skills and relationships. And don't hire people who are happy just being employees. Hire people who have an ownership mindset. One of the best indicators of future success of a new advisor coming into the business is any entrepreneurial experience in college or later in life. Someone with strong relationship-building abilities and business acumen.

Leaders with a growth mindset spend a lot of time looking outward. They pay attention to their competition.

They pay attention to business, economic, technological, and social trends. They pay attention to the world and they make a concentrated effort to experience the world through a variety of viewpoints. The more curiosity you have the more engaged and enjoyable the journey.

In Chapter 7, I discussed self-awareness. I asserted that great leadership starts with self-awareness. Self-awareness is not about navel-gazing. It is the starting point from which a leader acquires the tools with which to look outward.

All great leaders know this. Yet, not all organizations do this. My services are often used when organizations, large or small, seek to look outside of their own walls. They want to gauge their own sense of performance and find ways in which they can improve the client experience and thus their business results. Virtually all of their existing measurements are internal. As a result, they have no idea how they are doing relative to their competition.

Ask yourself:
- How is my firm doing relative to the competition?
- What are my main competitors doing in this market that's working? Should we be doing that as well?
- What are my main competitors doing in this market that's not working? Let's not do that!

Always keep an eye—better yet, both eyes—on your competition. Don't get complacent when you're doing well. Make it a habit to constantly evaluate what your competition is doing. You will learn from their successes. You will learn even more from their failures.

Spend the Time and Take Your Time

Everyone you recruit must be aligned with the vision, culture, and strategy of your organization—this goes for your receptionists and assistants as much as for your team leaders and managing directors. Recruit people who fit into the world-class service model that defines your brand.

While great leaders focus on recruitment, average managers don't spend nearly enough time identifying the right people who can help them grow the business. Not investing the necessary time and resources in recruitment is the single biggest mistake I see firms commit. Others include:

- Being too focused on selling the firm to the recruit versus selling yourself, how can you add value? What makes you different from other managers?
- Trying to do it all by yourself. Bring in and showcase your team.
- Not really listening to what's important to the recruit. Don't make assumptions. Is this person a good fit with your existing firm and team?

Addressing all of these mistakes is quite simple—it just takes time. I challenge you to spend considerably more time sourcing and identifying people who have the ability to adapt to the culture you have worked so hard to build.

> "First get the right people on the bus, the wrong people off the bus, and the right people in the right seats, and then they can figure out where to drive it."
>
> —*Jim Collins, Good to Great*

Always give the advisor the full story: the good, the bad, and possibly the ugly. Ask open-ended questions and then zip it up. Listen carefully. Listen as well for what's not being said. I always like to start from the beginning with, "Tell me about yourself: Where did you grow up?," and inevitably, "What's important to you over the next five years?" and "In managing your practice, what's your process and what's your investment philosophy?" I ask the question and then give my undivided attention to listen to the advisor's response.

You need to have a well-defined process. One of the biggest mistakes I see all the time is not recruiting from within your own office first. That's from where all subsequent introductions come. Retention is just as important as recruitment. As a manager, I knew if I could keep everyone happy that I would be successful.

I always emphasize the word *partners*. Being a good partner means we both have to keep our end of the promise, our commitments. If I am a good partner as the leader/manager, I'm going to create a great working environment, and if I can't do that, I become a poor partner. Advisors are smart, and they are also street smart and have a nose to sniff out when they are getting the short end of the stick. Ultimately, a good partnership has trust and collaboration. The manager goes to bat for the advisor, and most of the time it's not to help the advisor but to help the client.

Positive Attitude

You should have five reasons why someone should join your firm, whether working with you or for you. The best reason is the fact the you can help them grow their business. One of the most important things you can do as the leader is to help the advisor leverage the firm, to provide and connect the right people and resources within and from outside the firm. This alone can help the advisor grow her business and better serve her clients. Have a coaching process that works because you have developed the skills and have the capacity and competency to help. You have a great team that provides everyone with the right support. When they walk into the office, they are walking into the best environment. Everyone that's part of the support team is a superstar. If they're not, ask yourself why you allowed this to happen.

All Straight Talk

As I've said before, under-promise and over-deliver. Some people have short memories, so put as much as you can on paper. Be flexible, but don't compromise your integrity.

Keep Your Word and Follow Through

After you recruit someone, introduce him to the rest of the team as quickly as possible and again at your next meeting. Remember, when it comes to respect and loyalty you can't demand it; you have to earn it. Moving from one firm to another is extremely emotional not to mention difficult when trying to move an entire client base. For the first several weeks be sensitive to the emotional needs of the new hire. Some of my mistakes were not picking up clues of just how much stress the new advisor was feeling. The best clue is when someone tells you everything is going great and everyone is in a good spot. That's not usually reality. A big book brings even more complexity and issues to be worked out. I made it a point to say hello to all the new advisors at least twice a day, regardless of how large the office was, once in the morning and again in late afternoon. I made it a point of asking at least one question and my favorite was "What can I do to help you?"

Recruitment Is Just the Beginning

Once you have your talented people on board, you must continually add value, because that's the only way you can increase the probability that your attrition rate will be satisfactory. Adding value means different things to different people. Value for someone in the business for less than five years may be different than for someone in the business for 25 years. One size will not always fit all. Focus on what you can control in terms of the environment you're creating. Most people will appreciate that you made the effort. Remember: recruiting is a contact sport.

Chapter 10

Creating Outstanding Teams

"An empowered organization is one in which individuals have the knowledge, skill, desire and opportunity to personally succeed in a way that leads to collective organizational success."

—*Stephen Covey*

The future of an effective wealth management practice is not solely based on how good their strategy is, or how successful their asset allocation models are, or how advanced their technology is; it will be about attracting the right people who embrace teamwork. The ultimate competitive edge will be that firm, office, or team that makes teamwork part of the culture, vision, and strategy. It all starts with who is on the team, and if any member of the team prefers solo endeavors, it probably means the team is already at a disadvantage. My brother, who is also my best friend, loves to ride his Harley Davison. He logs about 20,000 miles a year.

He likes to ride alone because he doesn't have to compromise. If you ride with a group, you need to ride at the speed of the slowest rider. You may need to stop more often when in a group. You need to come to an agreement on destination. Therefore, my brother would rather ride alone most of the time. He clearly is a free spirit who marches to his own drum. For him, being on a team would be like cutting off his oxygen. On the other hand, if he found a few riders who shared his values, destination, endurance, and so on, the team approach would work for him.

The bottom line is that some people don't have the DNA to be a good teammate. Even those people who thrive in team situations still need to participate in the right training on a regular basis because things continually change. A team is always evolving and a team dynamic must continuously be cultivated. Getting a team to peak performance takes determination. Keeping a team in top form requires just as much determination. Why is it so hard? Because we are all different; we all have different styles, responses, and motivations. Doing whatever you want, when you want to and never having to be held accountable sounds attractive. But, when you're committed to playing your role on a team you can't have that attitude.

What helps to focus a team made up of different people with different drives is a united purpose and clearly defined roles. Why is the team doing what they're doing? What is the team hoping to solve? It can't just be about compensation. It needs to be about the client. Everyone needs to feel there is a common purpose. Look at any outstanding sports team—there is no denying that those teams that have a clear purpose play extremely well together. It's critical to clearly define performance expectations as well as openly discuss and resolve poor group performance.

Recruiting top talent is the key step in creating outstanding teams and creating outstanding teams is something leaders with a growth mindset do constantly and consistently. There's skill to establishing an outstanding team and not just putting people together and hoping for the best. Being on a team is not always easy. It sometimes means supporting another person, compromising, and communicating when you don't feel like it. Successful teammates must be flexible.

While there are plenty of situations in the wealth management industry over which we have little control, creating high-performing, successful teams is something we can definitely control.

Characteristics of an Elite Team

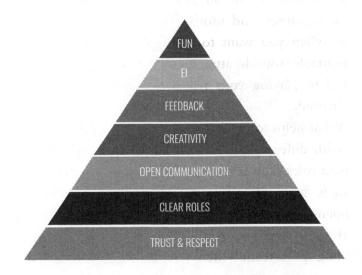

FUN

EI

FEEDBACK

CREATIVITY

OPEN COMMUNICATION

CLEAR ROLES

TRUST & RESPECT

Essentials of What Makes a Great Team

The members of a great team:

- Trust each other
- Respect each other
- Like each other
- Like to be successful and like to win

When clients are in front of a great team, they can feel it. It's like listening to a great band; you just know when they're making awesome music.

Elite Teams

In a BlackRock survey of elite RIAs, 44 percent of those surveyed indicated that their clients are served by a team rather than by an individual, as compared to other RIA firms in which only 30 percent of clients are served by a team. Instead, these RIAs assign almost half (49%) of their individual advisors to individual clients. Additionally, 74 percent of the elite RIAs indicated that they have an investment committee, compared with just 47 percent of all other financial firms, which rely on the traditional positions of a chief investment officer and senior research analyst. In the bank trust world, teams make the difference. While team-driven practices are not yet widespread and adopted by the majority of large firms, it is an emerging trend that I believe could represent a significant shift in the service models employed by some of the industry's largest and most elite firms.

The team approach to client service is a powerful differentiator. Specialized teams operating within any firm can provide better service and increase levels of expertise in the full scope of wealth management. Because of increased competition and greater demands on the high-net-worth client it's becoming increasingly more difficult for one person to wear all the hats of a comprehensive wealth management business.

Generally, teams are organized with four or five specialized roles: portfolio manager, financial planner, trust advisor, relationship manager, and business development officer. There are times when the relationship manager and business development officer are the same person.

The biggest challenge I see for such teams is maintaining a strong leadership process, or full ownership from start to finish. Most of the time everyone collaborates effectively, but when one person takes the leadership role from the discovery meeting into the ongoing service of that account, that makes the difference. Often it's the relationship manager who plays this role, a leader who not only has all the necessary skills to do a great job as the generalist, but also excels in the business development role. I see this as the biggest opportunity to take a team's effectiveness to new levels.

I would add another critical skill to the team leader's arsenal: coaching. The coach has a front-row seat every time the team is in front of a client and every time the team has a pre- and/or post-meeting debrief. If the coach is trusted and respected by the other team members and can make small improvements to the overall approach, style, and delivery, he or she can have a substantial impact on the team's performance.

Most firms are focused on helping advisors with soft skills and relationship or sales skills. In the past, advisors generally managed the portfolios and focused on relationship building with the client. However, this format is changing and will continue to evolve. Today's advisors are being asked to do more. They have to manage portfolios in the most efficient way possible to create greater capacity in order to spend more time deepening client relationships and increasing wallet share. Part of their compensation is also based on net asset growth. In short, the CFA designation is no longer sufficient; the advisor also needs the relationship, collaboration, and communication skills that can lead to outstanding performance for both the client and the team.

In the wirehouse or independent broker/dealer, a focus on teams has been steadily growing over the past 20 years, although there is still much to be done. From vertical teams to horizontal teams, some are more effective than others. Since we have an aging advisor population, teaming and succession planning is something that more organizations are implementing.

At the end of the day, what does this mean for the client? Is this for personal gain only? After many years of seeing different models across all the channels, I'm absolutely convinced that a highly effective team helps the client much more than a sole practitioner. When I asked one team, "What makes you different from others?" they were quick to respond by saying, "Because we work so well together we can deliver superior client service, comprehensive financial planning, an outstanding investment process, and strong performance."

Remember, it's not a team in and of itself that makes a firm different from others: it's a team that's effective, passionate, brilliant, and kind to each other and their clients.

An Elite Team

- Is all things to some people
- Fully leverages the firm
- Values speed and collaboration
- Delivers a disciplined wealth management process

On an Elite Team

- Everyone can articulate a clear belief and execution of his or her value proposition.
- Everyone is committed to delivering excellent client service and investment results based on the clients' objectives.
- Everyone is dedicated to new client acquisition and asset growth.
- Everyone proactively builds client loyalty.
- Everyone respects and trusts one another.
- Everyone is committed to improving; members challenge each other and ask for feedback.

Dysfunctional Teams

Successful teams help increase revenue growth, asset growth, profitability, market share, improve client and employee satisfaction. The only time a team doesn't make sense is when it's dysfunctional. Unfortunately, I believe that in the wealth management industry, most teams are not operating at their optimal level. Although many wealth management firms have good intentions about organizing as teams and team-building, too many of the teams are dysfunctional.

Teams are not effective when their members:

- Don't fully trust each other
- Don't fully respect each other
- Fear conflict
- Have different levels of commitment
- Spend little or no time on improvement
- Do not recognize each other
- Let individual egos get in the way
- Have poor communication skills
- Don't fully appreciate and understand the competition
- Don't value speed and have no sense of urgency
- Lack the passion and the appropriate skill set to add value
- Simply don't like being on a team

Most importantly, teams are ineffective when they don't have a clearly defined leader. I'm not talking about a leader whom they report to. I'm referring to the leader who's part of the engagement process.

When a team has no leader, there is no one to hold people accountable. How a team is structured—horizontal, vertical, situational, and so forth—is paramount to its success but highly idiosyncratic to the specific project or organization. What is never idiosyncratic is leadership. Every team needs a clearly defined leader.

Healthy Conflict

Healthy conflict involves communicating in a professional and generous manner. Outstanding teams have healthy debates and an unfiltered exchange of ideas and feedback.

Nobody walks on eggshells because everybody understands that conflict is vital to the success of the team. Diversity in thought will almost always result in a better client outcome.

Even though the word *conflict* might have negative connotations, healthy conflict is free of sarcasm, put-downs, and personal attacks. It is characterized by team members who respect one another, listen to gain understanding, and debate to find solutions. That's why emotional intelligence is so important. A team with low EI will always be struggling to improve.

Empowerment

Finally, and most importantly, great leaders empower their teams. They learn quickly that real power comes from others. It is by unleashing each individual's strengths that a leader can achieve extraordinary results. By empowering others, as a leader you show you are willing to share power. It shows you trust them. As a result, you can move with speed. Freedom and creativity come from a team that's empowered. Frameworks and boundaries are important but outstanding performance from a team is impossible without empowerment.

Consider this:
- Recognition is vital: recognize your team as people and not just advisors. Recognize them not just for production or asset growth, but also for things like achieving their personal best, reaching major milestones, and special events in their lives, such as an addition to the family. Did John just become a father? Celebrate John with his team. Recognize the right behavior, not just a successful outcome.

The Ideal Team Player
- Has a growth mindset
- Is humble
- Has a high IQ
- Is someone who can be trusted and respected
- Likes people
- Has confidence
- Is competent

Hierarchy for Who Delivers a Highly Customized Wealth Management Client Experience

A team that wins together also loses together and grows together. If the stakes are high enough, the team comes together much faster and works with greater collaboration. Make the stakes high, be bold, and climb a higher mountain. Focus on bigger relationships, ones that will stretch everyone. By doing so you will increase your performance. Finally don't fight the current. Don't try to force people to work together. Just like you can't beat a river into submission, stop wasting energy fighting the current. Stop wasting time trying to motivate those that are unmotivated. However, for those who are motivated, a great team working together will perform magic for the client relationship.

Chapter 11

Have the Courage to Lead Change

"Courage is what it takes to stand up and speak; courage is also what it takes to sit down and listen."

—*Winston Churchill*

Leaders with a growth mindset have courage. We all know this intuitively. But what does it really mean? For me, it means that they show their mettle in tough situations and they excel at making difficult decisions. It's showing your courage by your deeds, not just words. It becomes much more difficult to have courage to make the right decisions if you don't feel good about yourself as we discussed in managing yourself and self-care. Confidence may be the center key, but you need, skill, knowledge, experience, and the right attitude to move forward with courage.

Moving Through Fear

"The greatest pleasure in life is doing things people say
you cannot do."

—*Walter Bagehot*

Having courage does not mean never being afraid. It
means being able to act despite your fears. The more you
run away from your fears, the more they grow and the
more power you give them. Great leaders confront their
fears head-on. Visualize a successful outcome.

One of the fears I had early on in my career was a fear
of speaking in public. As an advisor, I desperately wanted to
lead seminars and I knew my fear of public speaking would
stop me from achieving this goal. To conquer my fear,
I started bringing in guest speakers for my seminars. At
first, I would simply introduce my guest to the group. Over
time, my introductions got longer and longer and eventually I became the main speaker.

Consider this:
 1. Name a fear you have.
 2. Ask yourself: What am I afraid of losing?
 3. Think of a way you can move through it.

Leadership requires courage because leadership requires
us to act according to what we believe is right, even when
it is difficult. Courageous leadership is the ability to operate without a safety net in order to serve our principles and
our values. Courageous leadership means doing the right
thing even when there is a personal or professional cost.

Ask yourself:
- What decisions or actions in my professional life require the most courage?
- Do I routinely act with courage, even when there is a personal or professional cost? Or do I compromise in the name of short-term peace?
- Do I have the courage to listen to, and to really hear, dissenting opinions from clients, advisors, and partners?

The Courage to Hire and Fire

Nowhere is courageous leadership more apparent than in the realm of hiring and firing talent. Have the courage to hire the right person for the job instead of the safe person. Unfortunately, in our field it is common for CEOs to replace their direct reports not with the best candidate but with the person who needs to be placated (for example, someone who has threatened to leave the firm). When making hiring choices, the most important thing you can do is to attract the right people for the right roles and hold them accountable—and that takes competence, confidence, and courage.

You need to have courage to fire people, too. If you make the hiring decisions, you will inevitably make some mistakes. But living with a mistake just because you made it only compounds it. There are many reasons why someone is not the right fit for the office or firm. Have the courage to do the right thing on behalf of the entire team and all stakeholders. A bad hire is a detractor from the culture you're trying to create. A friend of mine, one of the most experienced managers I have ever met, likes to remind leaders that people who work for you and people whom you report to are not your friends. You need to understand yourself that you're running a business; therefore, in spite of how much you like someone, don't confuse your job as a leader with "friendship." Be friendly and build relationships but remember they're not your friends. Personally, it took me a long time to truly understand that, because I tried to build deep, close relationships over time. But friendship can never stop you from serving all the stakeholders. Managers who operate that way just want to please everyone and be liked, but at the end of the day they are not running a business. As my friend would say, "We are not here to acquire new friends." It's not just about whom you hire or fire. It's about making the right decisions without getting overly emotional about the outcomes, which is certainly easier said than done.

Critical Insight: Leaders, Bullies, and Respect

Awareness about bullying has come a long way. However, it still exists today in corporate America. You may not want to label it *bullying*, and that's fine. Let's call it being disrespectful, or call it having an overinflated ego that causes others to feel very uncomfortable. Call it what you wish, but the leaders who are humble, respect others and admit mistakes will always outshine the narcissistic leader—they are servant-leaders. They don't abuse power; they give power. No *if*s, *and*s, or *but*s. When a leader walks into a room, he says, "There you are!" with enthusiasm. When a bully walks into a room, he says,

"Here I am. Look at me." Have the courage to stand up to bullies and those who are arrogant and disrespectful. If you don't, your regret for not standing up will never leave you. I have witnessed many arrogant bullies in my life and I blame the firms that tolerate that behavior.

Bullies cannot be tolerated in any organization. One bully is detrimental to an organization's entire culture, energy, and productivity, whether he or she is an advisor, manager, CEO, or client. Bullies do the following:

- Dominate and intimidate others
- Lack empathy
- Ridicule and demotivate others
- Surround themselves with people who acquiesce to them
- Lack the ability to trust people
- Withhold information
- Act in an aggressive and emotionally immature manner
- Tend to be hyper-focused on taking power, credit, and recognition
- Demand their followers serve them
- Exhibit selfish behavior by focusing on themselves rather than the team
- Are quick to judge
- Are often passive-aggressive
- Are unable to see other points of view
- Offer solutions based solely on their worldview
- Blame others for their failures

Tolerating bullies in your organization affects your profits and productivity. It is that simple. Eradicate them immediately.

Consider this:

- Have the courage of your convictions. If you work for a bully, calmly express how you feel and say why the bully's behavior is not appropriate. Stay cool and calm and, above all, professional. If the person continues with inappropriate behavior, go to human resources. No one should have to work for a bully. If you feel that that's the environment you're working in and you have seen that you are not able to change that culture, then you need to leave. And that takes courage.

One of the benefits of writing a book and being a speaker is the fact that you meet a lot of very smart, motivated, and passionate people. I have the highest respect for the people I have interviewed for this book. Dave Kelly is one of those smart executives who really gets it. I had the pleasure of meeting with Dave in his beautiful Toronto office in the TD tower. From the 35th floor the views are pretty cool. Dave leads the wealth businesses that serve high-net-worth Canadians for TD in Canada, about 1,200 advisors. He is one of those special individuals who can talk strategy and vision at the highest levels and also have that coaching-like conversation with a frontline advisor. Based on my experience most people in our business can't do both well.

The first thing that struck me about Dave was his humble style and the strong conviction of where the business is going. In the business 20 years, Dave said, "I have never seen change happening so fast." But he is embracing this change because he believes technology will enhance the client experience. He is also the first to launch a fully integrated high-net-worth wealth management offering with brokerage, private banking, private trust, and discretionary investment management aligned under one leadership structure. Over time he wants to move toward a truly client-centric team compensation model, and no doubt he knows that's a tricky task to tackle. In such a model, the investment advisor is the quarterback, the key relationship person.

Like most people, Dave believes to truly meet client needs you must deliver advice beyond investments. He feels the discovery meeting is by far the most important meeting and one an advisor should never delegate to someone else: "Value creation is in the discovery meeting. High-net-worth clients are not generally as price sensitive as other client segments, but they are very value sensitive." They are prepared to pay for advice and service that is highly valuable and valued. He went on to say that after 2008, clients' expectations on collaboration are much higher. He wants his advisors to find out "Who is important to you? What is important to you? And where are you trying to go as a family?" Therefore "the conversation is about a family's vision and values, not what they own and owe in dollars and cents. We need to understand how our clients think about wealth, risk, and what may cause them to deviate from their plan. For us, the challenge is how to simplify this conversation and the planning conversation for our clients and advisors."

When I asked Dave what he thought about robos, he said,

> Most advisors are anxious about robos and fintech; however, my view is that technology will help advisors deliver an even more compelling client experience. I think technology can change the current planning experience from a 98-page plan full of tables and charts [for

example, I had a financial plan done with Kim (Dave's wife) a couple of years ago and now I can't even tell you what room of my house it's in] to an ongoing digitally enabled, collaborative, simplified experience that will transform the planning conversations and experiences.

Dave believes that technology will help make these plans collaborative and dynamic and operate in real time. Future clients will have the ability to choose a robo, a direct investment advisor, or the full wealth management team.

> Clients can choose how collaborative they would like to be with an advisor for all elements of their wealth management experience. They may do elements of their investing themselves and others with advisors or fully entrust the investing decisions to a portfolio manager. Collaboration is here to stay and the new era will empower the client even more.

Dave is having a great year in terms of asset growth and attracting the right advisors. I asked him what it takes to be a leader in our business. Without hesitation he replied,

> We are in the hearts-and-minds business. Anyone can review a sales process or pipeline; it's all about your ability to influence. It's getting to the *how*. Unless you fundamentally enjoy herding cats, you're in the wrong business. If I tried to tell people what to do, I would surely see more of the universally recognized hand gestures letting me know they would not do as I say than I could count.

When thinking about his business, Dave focuses on the key building blocks: vision, strategy, communication, measurable metrics, aligned compensation, and reward and recognition. If just one block is out of alignment, nothing works. I asked Dave to describe his leadership challenges. He zeroed in on ownership of the vision, a commitment from all the leaders in the organization. One way Dave talks about gaining more credibility with advisors is the process of "discovery with advisors," in others words, truly getting to know the advisors, their investment philosophy, value proposition, and so on, and of course being fully transparent. "I look for the soft skills. This is a listening game, not a talking game. It's a question game, not a telling game. It's all about the caliber of the questions."

As you can see, Dave and I have the same worldview on virtually everything. Dave and I share the same opinion that having a particular title doesn't make you a leader. "Titles are irrelevant," Dave emphasizes. After his 90-minute reviews with his direct reports every month, he ends each meeting with, "What support do you need from me?"

Dave would describe the elite advisor as having the following qualities or skills:

> One, they have gained trusted advisor status with their clients; two, they have a clear vision of where they want to take their business; three, they have a plan with the team with clear roles; four, they can clearly articulate their investment philosophy; and five, they build a team to scale model portfolios and perhaps add a planner to

the team. In our business model we can't be successful unless we help our advisors to grow more quickly and more profitably than the competition, which you can only sustain through legendary client-and-employee experiences. Our role as leaders is to look three to five years ahead and plan accordingly. We need to ask ourselves what model high-net-worth Canadians will value and be willing to pay for.

I agree and believe it will be an integrated model.

I myself like to ask people, What do you worry about? Can we help advisors with this opportunity we see and are we ready to help enough advisors to make the shift? If that doesn't inspire you as a leader, you may want to read it again. Dave wants to win big. He leads by influence, not title. "Advisors will never listen if you talk at them." He feels culture rules the day and it's the one major competitive advantage. This culture is defined by what you do, not what you say. So, how does one win, I ask? "Be driven, be disruptive, and have diversity of thought." Dave goes on, "The challenge I put to the advisors is this: What is the last human capability and capacity that is hard to automate? Emotional connection and empathy. It's not asset allocation or picking stocks or running a plan."

Here are Dave's parting words of wisdom at the end of our conversation:

> When I'm in front of advisors who are thinking about moving from their firm, they are asking themselves, "If I look out five years, what model will win? Where do I need to be? Will they have the right leaders, the right culture, the right team?"

It was such a pleasure talking to Dave. It is clear he focuses on and executes all the right strategies because he understands that soft skills are what drive people.

A World of Possibilities and Opportunities

"The babies being born in America today are the luck-
iest crop in history. America's economic magic remains
alive and well."

−Warren Buffett

I discussed in the introduction of the book that change is happening faster than any time in recent history. There-fore, it goes without saying that leading change will be para-mount for the future manager or advisor. John P. Kotter, author of *Leading Change*, is renowned for his work on leading organizational change. His research says:

Unsuccessful transitions almost always founder during at least one of the following phases: generating a
sense of urgency, establishing a powerful guiding coa-
lition, developing a vision, communicating the vision
clearly and often, removing obstacles, planning for and
creating short-term wins, avoiding premature declara-
tions of victory, and embedding changes in the corporate culture.

Having the courage to lead change by definition means operating with some unknowns. For some this may be uncharted waters utilizing a new tool, new technology, or a different product or service. For many in the industry, roles are changing to focus more on building relationships versus time-consuming tasks that will eventually be handled by robots. Leading change could mean improving the culture or changing the business or wealth management model. At times leading change is simply about dealing with a crisis; it's about getting that unpleasant phone call on an idle Tuesday afternoon. Making change happen and dealing with change both require competence, confidence, and a strong vision.

During the 2008–2009 global financial crisis, I was the national sales manager at Morgan Stanley and I would be lying to you if I didn't tell you that in that position, I experienced more than my fair share of anxiety. I kept myself glued to the talking heads on various cable networks and read several newspapers every morning. Everyone working in financial services knows it was a very scary time, for our clients as well as ourselves.

In the middle of all the chaos and fear, one person stood out from the crowd by showing courage, confidence, and optimism for the future. That person was investor extraordinaire Warren Buffett. As virtually everyone else panicked, Buffett remained calm and took a long-term view.

Warren Buffett's reaction to the crisis and his confidence that we would weather the storm gave me a sense of peace and hope. His optimism shined even brighter because things were so uncertain. Warren Buffett understood the profound need, as a leader, to calmly navigate through an incredible crisis. He showed more than optimism. He showed wisdom.

Experienced advisors with decades of experience also taught me about courage and a sense of perspective. These wise advisors were like master sailors; they understood the challenges of a rough sea. But, more importantly, they knew how to navigate their clients through this once-in-a-lifetime storm. They had the courage to stay calm, and didn't panic and sell at the bottom. What did they have that others didn't? What did they know that others couldn't see? They had a perspective based on history, they had lived through life experiences, they never gave up hope, they were well-read, they were laser-focused on their clients, and they over-communicated with everyone, from clients and their team to partners and managers. They had the courage to be proactive versus go into hiding.

Examine Your Assumptions

As a self-made, rather than born, optimist, I find it helpful and necessary to intermittently examine my beliefs, values, and assumptions. Where's my mindset? What are my go-to beliefs, values, and assumptions? Am I holding onto beliefs that are keeping me from moving forward? Making assumptions that a team is operating just fine or that performance seems okay holds you back. If you hold the belief, "If it's not broken, don't mess with it," it probably means your forward momentum has stalled. Or, if you believe that it's better not to get involved in difficult situations because things will just take care of themselves—you're probably stuck. Neither one of these beliefs is part of a growth mindset. Unfortunately, we come across these sentiments all the time.

The Greater the Confidence, the Greater the Courage to Move Forward

I have found more often than not most successes start with confidence and end because of the lack of confidence. Sports is the best example.

There's a necessary balance to confidence because too much and you become arrogant. When I see a team or advisor in front of a client with a modestly sized portfolio, the confidence is at one level; yet when they are in front of a client outside their comfort level, while they may act confidently, they really are not. When you move through life with confidence, you open yourself to new possibilities and opportunities. How many times have we seen coaches berate children or leaders address their staff in ways that destroyed their confidence? Undoubtedly we've all seen that many times. And you know what happens next: fear and a lack of confidence keeps anyone playing it safe. Being in the safe zone is no way to go through life.

As a leader one of the great gifts that you can give someone is the confidence to move closer to his potential or the confidence to try something new. It's the only way to break out of fear. As poet E. E. Cummings said, "Once we believe in ourselves, we can risk curiosity, wonder, spontaneous delight, or any experience that reveals the human spirit." Instill in others the confidence they are looking for, even if they don't know it.

I work on being confident. If I make a mistake, I'm not very forgiving of myself. But there are a number of things I recommend to stay optimistic and confident:

- Kill negative self-talk. That little voice gets louder. Slay that dragon and live above it.
- Know who you are and what your principles are.
- Increase your competence.
- Set small goals and achieve them.
- Don't get overly emotional.

- Be grateful.
- Exercise.
- Empower yourself by mastering something.
- Look for people who will help your confidence; we all can use a cheerleader once in a while.
- Never stop moving forward. When one door closes, knock on a different one. If that door doesn't open, move to the next. A champion never loses enthusiasm.
- Don't allow criticism to live longer than it needs to in your head. That's precious real estate. Fill it with good thoughts.

Possibility-killing beliefs that tend to creep into the minds of leaders in our industry often include thoughts and ideas that do nothing except drain our energy:

- The belief that doing nothing is the best solution.
- It's impossible to be a top performer and have work/ life balance.
- Coaching advisors doesn't work.
- I don't have the resources I need.
- I can't get back to where I was.
- My boss doesn't value me or recognize my contribution.
- I don't have enough time to spend with my family or on business development.
- I'm in a terrible market for high-net-worth investors.

You need to stop this negative self-talk because your thoughts influence your actions. When you become aware of such negativity, acknowledge its existence, consider its damaging long-term effects, and proactively move forward.

If you begin with a sense of humility about your own skills and abilities, you will usually be curious enough to seek ways to improve your knowledge base and skill set. You will be drawn to seek growth.

If you're not actively seeking growth, personally or professionally, and are coasting instead, resting on your past accomplishments or acting mostly out of habit, it's time to shake things up. This stagnation can easily happen after 25 years in the business—it can easily happen with just a few years under your belt. When was the last time you did something that scared you? Have the courage to test yourself once in a while. Have the courage to lead change when others are playing it safe by the shoreline. No growth comes from playing not to lose.

Chapter 12

Leaders Are Grateful and Win Hearts and Minds

"At times our own light goes out and is rekindled by a spark from another person. Each of us has cause to think with deep gratitude of those who have lighted the flame within us."

—*Albert Schweitzer*

Leaders with a growth mindset don't go it alone and they are grateful to all the people who help them along the way. The awareness that they owe their success to the helping hands and support of others is a defining characteristic of all the great leaders I've had the privilege to work with. For me, gratitude is also the key identifier of leadership potential in new talent.

Consider this:
- Make a list of the people who've helped you in your career.
- Make a list of the people who've helped you achieve success or made a difference in your life.
- Think of clients that have gone out of their way to help you.
- If your list has fewer than a dozen names on it, think again, and again.

I would not have been able to build the career I have without the help of many people. I believe that to be true for every successful person. A sense of gratitude helps keep you grounded and humble. It also helps connect you in a powerful and meaningful way to the people you are leading and serving. Gratitude is a constant reminder that you are not the master of the universe. It is important to acknowledge the contribution of others in your success and to give back.

Ask yourself:
- Are you a giver or a taker? We can all improve and be more of a giver. Give more recognition. Give more value. Give more to those who need you inside and outside your office. Give more quality time to those you care about.

Consider this:
- Write a thank-you note to someone who has made a difference in your life. (*Note*: A thank-you note, not an email.)
- Consider making this a regular practice: something you do, with gratitude and humility, once a month.

If you model this way of operating, a significant part of your team will start to operate the same way and you will have sown the seeds of an incredible culture.

Narcissism Is Not Your Friend

I applauded Muhammad Ali's roar, "I am the greatest!" and I did not question either his athletic prowess or his showmanship. But "I am the greatest!" is not the roar of a great leader. In any leadership role, a large component of staying focused and managing to a greater purpose is the ability to see past labels and let go of any need to be viewed as important, or to be more respected and recognized than your peers.

These are elements of a stage performance, or one's own pride, but not of strong leadership. A great leader never has to say, "I'm a terrific leader." His or her actions speak volumes. Accolades and acknowledgment will come and go—one day we get them, the next day we don't. Stay true to the very best person you really are—that's enough.

Pride will never serve you as well as humility. Authenticity and cultivating your sense of gratitude are the best ways of staying rooted in humility and reality.

Influence

"The key to successful leadership is influence, not authority."

—*Kenneth H. Blanchard*

The ability to wield influence, not power, and the ability to inspire action are defining characteristics of leaders with a growth mindset. If you can't win hearts and minds or if you don't at least enjoy the challenge, you should find a different business. If you're an advisor, manager, or wholesaler, that's our job.

It may seem logical to want more power in your organization or career but great leaders focus on expanding their influence. Power is about allocating resources, and making and enforcing decisions. Influence is the mechanism through which people use power to change behavior or attitudes. Unlike power, influence can effect change without an obvious exertion of force, compulsion, or direct command.

> "The ability to influence is the key to being a great leader."
> —*From Power, Influence, and Persuasion*
> *(Harvard Business School Press)*

In a sense, influence is power with a velvet glove. That's why people without a title, who have no formal power, can influence people, decisions, and organizations as much as, and often more than, someone who holds an official position.

Persuasion

Persuasion is closely related to influence. It is a process through which one aims to change or reinforce the attitudes, worldviews, opinions, or behaviors of others.

> "There is a profound difference between management and leadership and both are important. 'To manage' means 'to bring about, to accomplish, to have charge of or responsibility for, to conduct.' 'Leading' is 'influencing,

guiding in direction, course, action, opinion.' . . . An essential factor in leadership is the capacity to influence."

—*Warren Bennis and Burt Nanus,*
Leaders: Strategies for Taking Charge

Since the beginning, most businesses have operated with the help of power, influence, and persuasion. Aristotle knew this 2,300 years ago when he boldly identified that logic and reason are not sufficient to the arts of influence and persuasion. Logos, pathos, and ethos—logic, emotions and character—must work together. This is the magic of influence and the magic of leadership: it works on not only the minds of an audience, but also their hearts.

Despite millennia of knowledge and insight into the velvet power of influence, managers young and old still try to use power to get things done, thinking, "I'm the boss, I know better— I have the power to make them do what I want or else."

"Never expect anyone to engage in a behavior that serves your values unless you give that person adequate reason to do so."

—*Edward Dwyer*

It doesn't work. But influence does.

"Power/Influence is the ability to get people to perceive that a given behavior (or performance) is the best action they can take in service of their values."

—*Edward Dwyer*

I hope you are connecting the dots. Being grateful and not arrogant helps you in so many ways in building a business not to mention living your life. When you are networking, leading your team, creating a culture, collaboration and so on you simply travel lighter through life.

SUMMARY: Part One

Leaders with a Growth Mindset Grow

To succeed in the wealth management business, you need to add value and earn trust every day. The plan is to be a student of the business, to grow as a leader, and to cultivate a growth mindset. Are you ready?

- Growth starts with self-awareness and working on increasing emotional intelligence, and leaders with a growth mindset cultivate such self-awareness. They know themselves and they know their strengths as well as their weaknesses. They start with a vision and purpose.

- A growth mindset requires good energy. Great leaders take care of themselves.

  "Your first and foremost job as a leader is to take charge of your own energy and then help to orchestrate the energy of those around you."

  —*Peter Drucker*

- A growth mindset is rooted in credibility. Great leaders have credibility and work hard to stay credible.
- Leaders with a growth mindset are grateful and humble. Practicing gratitude and humility keeps them curious, always learning, and, as a result, adaptable.

  "I am an optimist. It does not seem too much use being anything else."

  —*Winston Churchill*

- Growth inspires and is inspiring: leaders with a growth mindset inspire by example.
- A growth mindset is characterized by optimism and a sense of possibility. Great leaders live in a world of possibility and they take their people into this world.
- Growth is impossible without communication and leaders with a growth mindset are great communicators. This means they are great listeners as well as compelling storytellers.
- Leaders with a growth mindset wield influence, not power.
- Growth is impossible without collaboration. Leaders with a growth mindset collaborate effectively.
- A leader with a growth mindset constantly creates and works toward fulfilling shared visions.

- Leaders with a growth mindset have courage. They show their mettle in tough situations and they excel at making difficult decisions.

"Whenever you see a successful business, someone once made a courageous decision."

—*Peter Drucker*

- A growth mindset thrives in strong organizational cultures. Leaders with a growth mindset are committed to creating those cultures.
- A leader with a growth mindset recognizes the need to recruit, nurture, and deploy the talent of others.
- A growth mindset empowers others and empowerment is the first step in creating outstanding teams.
- Leaders with a growth mindset have a strong sense of personal responsibility. They take responsibility for their past, present, and future. They are fully aware of what they are creating, promoting, and allowing.
- Leaders with a growth mindset invest in the growth of others. They are focused on being effective coaches.

Leaders with a growth mindset pay attention to the world and they make an effort to view the world through a variety of points of view.

"Twenty years from now you will be more disappointed by the things that you didn't do than by the ones you did do. So throw off the bowlines. Sail away from the safe harbor. Catch the trade winds in your sails. Explore. Dream. Discover."

—*Mark Twain*

PART TWO

Growing Your Wealth Management Business

O ver the past 30 years, the wealth management industry has experienced phenomenal growth as well as a profound transformation. As I discussed in Part One, the catalysts of this transformation include the rise in client needs, greater levels of client sophistication, more investment choices, advanced technology, automated advice, and increased regulatory presence. Yet with all these changes, the advice business will continue to grow and flourish. It will evolve with machines and humans working together. Digital labor will only accelerate and be a major factor in how we manage money, relationships, and our time. I believe over the next 10 years the global wealth management industry will behave like a global geological system. The wealth management tectonics will cause disruption on a grand scale and will reshape the advisory landscape as we know it today. Advisors who feel they are on the hamster wheel running hard and not making any progress will feel even greater pressure because they will lose more ground. Therefore, don't wait until you lose that big relationship for your wakeup call. Start now. The secret is learning and evolving in real time.

Part Two of this book is all about growing assets, generating revenue, and building client loyalty. Growing the business starts with a conscious decision to effectively run the two parts of your business. One is managing the business and the other is growing it. If you're a sole practitioner, you must make asset growth part of your daily plan. Your foundation is great service and valued advice, but your book will not grow just because you show up and take care of your clients. To grow 10 or 20 percent or more (not including market appreciation/depreciation) you need to spend 40 percent of your time on business development activities. If you're part of a team, that 40 percent may be allocated to different members based on roles and responsibilities. Growing your practice is not a passive activity; it's a deliberate act of allocating time, investing resources, and being innovative. Yet the fact of the matter is that most advisors spend very little time hunting for new clients. Why? Because complacency sets in. For those who are serious about growth, I provide the roadmap in Part Two.

I see 11 ways to grow your business:

- If you have the resources to buy assets you should. Because of an aging advisor population this is an area that should not be overlooked. It takes a lot of time, patience, and research, not to mention money, to identify the right opportunities.

- Recruit quality advisors. Recruiting a junior advisor on your team can have a major impact.
- Ask clients for introductions. This is the most cost-effective way to grow. Over 50% of new business comes from introduction.
- Create strategic alliances.
- Focus on Centers of Influence (COIs) and networking.
- Target marketing programs.
- Host client events.
- Create a client board of advisors.
- Present seminars.
- Join a team or expand your team.
- Leverage social media.

Every one of these 11 strategies requires four things: a growth mindset, a willingness to invest back into the business, a competent team, and most of all the discipline to stay with the plan. For example, you wake up one day saying you will focus on seminars and after two seminars you conclude it doesn't work. It works if you are committed for 12 months with a plan and right strategy. The same is true for all business development activities; you can't start and stop. Just like diets don't work but changing your lifestyle does. The best advisors in our industry haven't just embraced the changes transforming wealth management but have turned the speed of business change to their advantage. As a result they are always focused on business development, employing new technology to automate processes, outsourcing where possible to create more capacity, and spending more time with clients and prospects. The future will demand that you take advantage

Business Growth Model

of technology to reduce the "busy" work. If you enjoy spending time doing something an algorithm can do, you will slowly become less relevant.

Start with your purpose; what are you hoping to accomplish? That will lead into vision. Business development doesn't happen unless you have a strong "why." Just for the record, business plans work; therefore, that's a good place to start. Incorporate a life plan as well, one that must be focused and monitored on an ongoing basis. A life plan should be a dynamic and a collaborative effort. It is your blueprint. It should not be more than three or four pages long. The following chapters should give you the information you need to build a customized plan. Start with one-year and three-year goals. Client retention, service excellence, team structure, business development, and expanding the client relationship are some examples. Are you the primary advisor for your 50 clients? If not, why not? What steps can you take to become the primary advisor? What additional advice, service, and solutions can you provide? Remember the core of wealth management is to build relationships based on a well-developed and fully integrated plan for achieving long-term wealth goals.

Chapter 13

Define Your Business Model

"If you are lucky enough to find a way of life you love, you have to find the courage to live it."

—*John Irving*

The term *wealth management* has become mainstream. It is used everywhere I travel, in leadership meetings of private client firms, in newspaper articles, and by advisors around the world. The term itself can be misleading. With more than 300,000 financial advisors in the United States alone, I have asked many professionals and clients over the past 10 years to describe what wealth management means to them. To no one's surprise, everyone describes it differently, and those descriptions often depend on what training you had, what firm you're with, and the business model you operate under.

There is a very wide spectrum of wealth management services depending on the level of one's wealth. Therefore, it's vital that before you start to think about the different ways to grow your business, you must think about what business model you want to build or expand. Will your firm support this model? For example, if financial planning is one of your core value propositions going forward, it's important to know the firm you're with has an appropriate platform. The $1 million relationships will have different needs and services than the $20 million relationships. As those assets grow, more complexity comes into play and, therefore, a highly competent and skilled team with specialized expertise is necessary. So, where is your sweet spot for your target market? Remember, if you are not the primary advisor on the relationship, you're always vulnerable. If you don't have all of that client's assets, you should use all the tools available to you to understand the goals and purposes of those various assets. You want to be able to see the whole picture, not just a piece of the pie. Based on what clients have told us for decades, they value great service, performance based on achieving their goals, fee transparency and value for what they pay for, and to be treated holistically. Your model must be based on what the client needs.

According to Bain & Company in the report, "Winning in Wealth Management," global wealth management is a big market in motion. Roughly speaking, investable assets are spread evenly across North America, Europe, and Asia-Pacific, but the challenges in each region could not be more different. Five nations represent more than half of the $101 trillion total, with the U.S. alone accounting for nearly $30 trillion. But asset growth in these markets remains low, at single-digit rates. By contrast, the dynamic markets of Asia and Brazil are growing at a rapid pace off a much smaller asset base.

Regardless of your client's level of wealth, you must clearly define how you will help them reach their goals. You should be able to clearly outline those steps and philosophies and create the infrastructure to put them into action. If you truly are delivering real wealth management services, your model should have the following pillars and the right team of experts. It's difficult if not impossible for one person to have all the disciplines. Being holistic and consultative means you start with a life plan. This life plan should include:

- Investment management
- Retirement planning
- Income protection
- Estate planning
- Family healthcare planning

Here is my top-10 list to help high-net-worth clients reach their goals:

   1. Create a comprehensive life plan. Helping clients determine if they need $5 million for a comfortable retirement is not a plan. The majority of investors don't have an actual life plan. Some firms charge $15,000 for a comprehensive plan while others include it as part of their services. The purpose of this plan is to help your clients define their vision and overall goals and create a strategic and tactical plan that will be executed over time. This plan must be dynamic, just like our lives.

2. If the client is still working, encourage him or her to deposit money directly into a retirement account. Taking advantage of corporate retirement plans can be a significant contributor to one's overall assets. However, how many clients keep these assets in fixed income or money market securities is astonishing to me.

3. Wealth management is not only about asset growth but also about asset preservation and asset transfer. Work with your clients to create a workable budget, whether they have $2 million or $20 million. I have witnessed people spend $10 million after retiring, and then run out of money because of their poor spending habits. Some people don't have financial discipline, which is why a budget is so critical. Determine what money means to the client; behavior toward money can be a key indicator in determining an appropriate plan.

4. It's always better to be debt-free. Include ways in which the client can reduce her taxes into her comprehensive plan and review them annually.

5. Help your clients decide an appropriate plan for their real estate assets. Is having three homes the right

long-term plan? Do they own too much house now? The average home size has increased by more than 1,000 square feet in the past 40 years, from an average size of 1,660 square feet in 1973 to 2,670 in 2013. Ask questions to help the client be realistic about what will suit her needs and budget.

6. Be boring (it's not, really) and play the long game. Managing expectations is key. Overall, an equity portfolio can be expected to perform well in the long run. As well, clients want value; therefore the advisor needs to pay attention to fees and help clients achieve the best value for their money.

7. Helping clients retire successfully is something that will separate good advisors from the mediocre herd. I'm not talking about just helping them hit a specific dollar number. I mean helping them map out what they will do after retirement. Make contingencies for when plans get derailed by an illness, job loss, or some life-changing event. Many ease into retirement by transitioning into part-time work.

8. Get the whole family involved. Generally, one person is usually responsible for managing the nest egg. That's a mistake, however, because if or when this person dies, the rest of the family may be in the dark and the learning curve to get up to speed could take years. I have seen this happen repeatedly. Make sure your client's children are a part of the discussions.

9. Make sure the client's full team—CPA, attorney, financial planner, and so on—are up to speed and working

in concert. You create tangible value when you help simplify the client's life.

10. Help your client network with other friends and clients for business opportunities or simply because they share a similar interest.

As you can see, investment management is only part of the model. Think about your model and write down your process, your experiences, and so on. What is your top-10 list?

Your Vision Should Inspire You to Take Action

Successful advisors know who they are, where they want to go, and how they plan to get there; they know their target market. The key to their success is simple: they do not attempt to be all things to all people; rather, they are all things to some people. They do not attempt to market themselves to a mass audience. We are operating in an overcrowded arena in which everyone becomes your competitor, including robos. Focusing your expertise with laser-like precision both reduces your competition and helps you to effectively target your defined market. You need to be very clear on how you plan to create a sustainable business model for growth.

Integrated Wealth Management

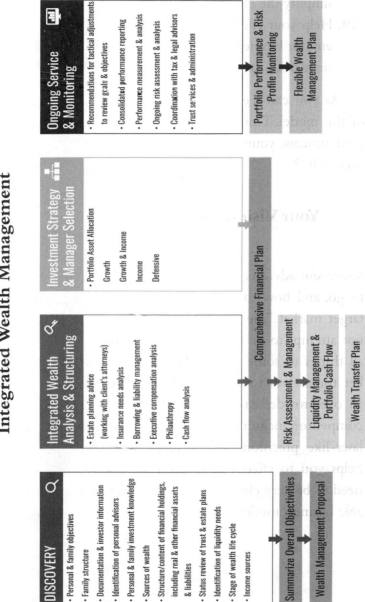

DISCOVERY

- Personal & family objectives
- Family structure
- Documentation & investor information
- Identification of personal advisors
- Personal & family investment knowledge
- Sources of wealth
- Structure/content of financial holdings, including real & other financial assets & liabilities
- Status review of trust & estate plans
- Identification of liquidity needs
- Stage of wealth life cycle
- Income sources

Summarize Overall Objectivities

Wealth Management Proposal

Integrated Wealth Analysis & Structuring

- Estate planning advice (working with client's attorneys)
- Insurance needs analysis
- Borrowing & liability management
- Executive compensation analysis
- Philanthropy
- Cash flow analysis

Comprehensive Financial Plan

Risk Assessment & Management

Liquidity Management & Portfolio Cash Flow

Wealth Transfer Plan

Investment Strategy & Manager Selection

- Portfolio Asset Allocation
  Growth
  Growth & Income
  Income
  Defensive

Ongoing Service & Monitoring

- Recommendations for tactical adjustments to review goals & objectives
- Consolidated performance reporting
- Performance measurement & analysis
- Ongoing risk assessment & analysis
- Coordination with tax & legal advisors
- Trust services & administration

Portfolio Performance & Risk Profile Monitoring

Flexible Wealth Management Plan

Know Your Model

The first step in growing your business is to define your business model. Be very clear about your core competencies, investment philosophy, service model, and marketing strategy. Always start by answering the "Why?," when it comes to the purpose and vision of what you want to achieve. Next, answer the "What?"—the goal or endgame of what you hope to achieve. Once you have a clear process and you've correctly branded the "authentic you," you'll find yourself in a much better position to know your value, articulate it, and price it accordingly.

Clients tend to ask prospective wealth managers the same key questions. Your response to these questions is what differentiates you from the thousands of other advisors out there. Interested prospects will want to know:

- "What business are you in?"
- "What makes you different?"
- "What processes or strategies would you use with my total financial picture?"
- "How are you going to accomplish my goals?"

And once your business vision is in place, self-reflection does not end. It's a continual process of evaluation and assessment and reevaluation and reassessment. On a regular basis (e.g., whether yearly or every five years, the time frame is for you to determine) ask yourself:

- What business am I really in? (Do I still enjoy getting up every day?)
- What business would I prefer to be in? (What changes should I make?)

- Have I built the right infrastructure for my practice?
- What's missing from my practice or life that will help me reach greater success?
- What am I creating, promoting, and allowing that's affecting my growth in business or in life?
- Am I reinvesting back into the business to keep up with technology?

The answers to these questions enable you to stay conscious of what's truly important to you, as well as be aware of what you are hoping to accomplish in both your professional and personal life.

The master in the art of living (according to a Zen Buddhist text) makes little distinction between:

- His work and his play
- His labor and his leisure
- His mind and his body
- His education and his recreation

Demonstrate Value

One question I often get in our current environment of fee compression is, "What's one of the best ways that an advisor can demonstrate value?" The short answer is to offer valued holistic advice and an exceptional client experience. Start by doing the unexpected. Do things clients and prospects don't expect, but which give you an opportunity to impress them. Filtering and contextualizing information is paramount. We live in a world of information overload, so the advisor's job is to provide a perspective on all that information.

We live in a world of tangible and intangible value. There are certain things of value that you can actually see, but there are even more that you can't but that you accept are there. What advisors have to remember about intangible value is it requires them to consistently demonstrate, communicate, and quantify that value to each client on a regular basis. And remember, clients and prospects may forget what you said in a meeting or review, but they will always remember how you made them feel. Those soft skills again.

The wealth management industry is large and competitive. But among the highest ranks—as suggested by feedback from more than 400 advisors there is little competition in this well-differentiated market. As a result, these advisors experience substantial growth year after year.

Important Factors for Selecting an Advisor

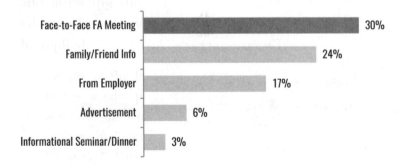

The true wealth manager analyzes the client's entire financial picture and focuses on asset accumulation, asset preservation, and asset transfer depending on the specialized needs involved. Therefore, the right wealth management model consists of a team that is competent in all the key areas of financial planning, portfolio management, estate planning, banking, and lending. Although there are many successful sole practitioners, it can be increasingly difficult for one individual to deliver a complete range of wealth management solutions, grow his or her business at double-digit returns, and still maintain quality of life.

In general, the bank and trust firms have a good process with a dedicated team in contrast to the wirehouse model in which clients may only work with one advisor. However, more and more wirehouses are building teams. Today, the strength, and simultaneously the challenge, of the wirehouse model is the fact that it consists of 56,000 entrepreneurs, each working independently. Therefore, they have individuals with a wide range of experiences, processes, team structures, and so forth. The wirehouse model needs to evolve faster to catch up with where the industry is headed. With improved technology, greater empowerment given to the local manager and advisor will better serve the client. The independent and RIA channels are the fastest growing and will continue to take market share because these advisors have more control over the way they run their business and have the opportunity to build their own brand, not to mention building equity.

Whatever business model you choose, it's important to focus on your value proposition and follow a systematic approach to meeting your goals. Cary Greenspan of PNC was kind enough to talk with me about his experiences and what he sees for the future of the industry.

Rick: Please tell me a little about yourself and your role at PNC.

Cary: I will very soon be entering my 35th year of continuous investment and portfolio management experience. After graduating with an MBA, I followed a slightly unconventional MBA path, becoming a stockbroker with Kidder, Peabody and Company in Washington, D.C. I also started an RIA and had various positions over the years. Today I serve on many executive committees for the PNC Asset Management Group. To name a few, I am a member of the Investment Policy Committee, the Investment Advisor Research Committee, and the Derivatives Policy Committee. My primary responsibilities include but are not limited to contributing to the overall investment thought leadership within PNC. This would include contributions and thoughts related to overall economic and financial conditions, how asset classes may be likely to perform, and how investment solutions are likely to provide a benefit or a detriment to client portfolios. I am also ultimately responsible for the fiduciary manner in which investment officers manage their portfolios.

Rick: You have been working with high-net-worth individuals for a long time. How do you see the business evolving going forward?

Cary: As in many industries, technology and access to information has become extraordinarily friendly to the entire investment client base. Lower costs, access to information, and the relative ease by which an investor can discover investment solutions or assistance to investment questions has made fee compression a challenge across all facets of the industry. In general, I see this trend continuing. The continual evolution of better products, easier access, and general solutions that will suit most investors' objectives will keep prices low. Even high-net-worth investors have significantly more options available to them now than ever before. Firms that make a concerted effort to fully understand the client's *personal* need and not their superficial and obvious financial need will be able to not only retain current clients but obtain significantly more clients who are otherwise somewhat indifferent to providers. Firms that offer no compelling personal or professional difference will force themselves into price reductions as they will offer no distinguishable advantages. Companies that suggest that client service is *the* primary focus often do not understand what they are measuring or how to deliver service to a client so that the client *feels* the value delivered. Investors who truly can feel different about their relationship with a provider will be completely engaged and truly dedicated to that firm and to those specific officers who provide that personal and professional assistance.

Rick: When it comes to core competencies, what do you think are the essential skills for an advisor in the future to be successful?

Cary: In part of a training program I both participated in and eventually taught, two questions would be asked at the outset to all participants. The first question was, "What was your major in college?" The second question was, "Knowing what you now know about this business, what major would you have wanted to study in college that would help you most now?" Typically 60 to 70 percent of the respondents to the first question had a technical major: business, finance, accounting, economics, pre-law, math, and so on. The answer for the second question (in the same percentages to the first question) was psychology, sociology, psychotherapy, and so on. I provide the anecdote to once again distinguish technical skill sets from interpersonal and personal skill sets. A person employed in wealth management or asset management must possess the technical knowledge base required to make sound judgments and offer practical advice. This is an absolute. Our business has thousands of incredibly intelligent JDs, CFAs, CPAs, CFPs, and other equally impressive credentialed professionals who provide remarkably similar and remarkably good counsel. But that does not always make the client feel that value has been achieved. Every client expects that he or she will be provided cogent and sound advice. And rightly so. But clients might receive the same advice and service next door for a lower fee. At what point do we assist the client with developing his or her sense of value and the personal dedication that we have as a company and as a person? The future skill set that is required is one of interpersonal skills and relationship development. Companies and individuals that invest in developing these skills will be far ahead of other competitors.

Rick: From the client's perspective in creating a positive client experience, what does that look like?

Cary: As I said earlier, clients rarely distinguish one provider from another until a relationship has developed. For the moment, if you remove the client aspect and only consider your own personal relationships, do you automatically trust someone you have just met, much less trust him or her completely? Don't you need some time to develop a trust between you and someone else? Granted this is a different circumstance. But the point to consider is that a client experience must go through stages like any relationship would. A client, however, has some formality associated with our actions. This is about setting expectations and meeting expectations. How often have we mishandled a new relationship and felt the sting of that for an extended period of time? Formal relationships require extraordinary communication and dedicated care. This cannot be left to chance. Clients know they have choices and new clients are now more vulnerable than ever before. Creating not only a positive client experience but a distinguishable, even remarkable client experience is how you add value. This is how a client will remember you. This is how a client will want to stay with you. And it is how you will obtain new clients. Your clients will be thrilled with their experience because it is not a common occurrence. Appropriate and adequate advice, adequate communication, and adequate performance is a general client expectation. Being able to excel in one of these three areas will foster a tremendous relationship. Executing on all three will create a multigenerational client with hundreds of friends and colleagues to follow.

Chapter 14

Business Development

Introductions

"Everyone wants to live on top of the mountain, but all the happiness and growth occurs while you're climbing it."

—*Andy Rooney*

Let me start with the good news, of the 300,000 advisors in the United States, the majority are not actively prospecting. A small percentage have a business development process, and even a smaller percentage are rainmakers that can produce significant asset growth on a consistent basis. The bad news is the fact that clients have many more choices and access to any information at their fingertips. Therefore being casual about business development is a waste of time and will only lead to frustration. Become committed to the art and science of growing the business,

163

but only if that's truly what you are committed to. The most important aspect of developing your business in an efficient and effective way is asking for introductions. But before you start to initiate a referral campaign, get your house in order. Because if your clients are not satisfied it will only result in disappointment. On the other hand it could serve as a wakeup call. It doesn't matter if you're just starting out or a 30-year industry veteran. About 60 percent of new business comes from referrals. That's an average; for some advisors it's 95 percent, for some it's 10 percent, and for others it's zero. I firmly believe introductions need to be a key component of business strategy, part of your culture and part of who you are. Based on my research, the following are the top five ways to focus on business development: introductions, strategic alliances, COIs and networking, target marketing programs, and client events.

Here is the myth of business development: if I'm really smart and provide great service, my business will grow naturally. As you know by now, I have met thousands of advisors over the years and that's simply not true. This business doesn't reward you for just being smart; there are lots of very smart people on Wall Street. The business or clients for that matter don't care how smart you are until you turn that body of knowledge into action. I have hired PhDs who failed quickly because they tried to outsmart the process of building a business. Business development rewards people who can execute, who are doers, and who are masters at networking. It rewards those that take some risks by trying new methods of growing their book. Most of all they persevere.

If you're thinking as an owner, you're always thinking about growing the business, not just managing the business. Growing the business means a commitment of time and resources.

There are a number of high-payoff activities you can facilitate to strengthen your client base and keep growing your business. These include:

- Hosting client events
- Arranging introductions
- Strategic networking
- Talking to clients/prospects
- Meeting with partners frequently
- Holding face-to-face reviews with clients/prospects

The following nine attributes make a rainmaker:

1. Self-confidence. A champion fails, but gets back up.
2. Great communicator and collaborator. Rainmakers ask great questions.

3. Lives in the world of possibilities, not limitations. They have a purpose and are motivated.

4. Takes full responsibility versus being a victim. They set business goals and activities and track progress.

5. High likability index. Humility attracts people.

6. They are competitive, they like to win. They are always prospering and networking.

7. They know what they don't know.

8. Relentless about details and follow-up. They have a sense of urgency. They know how to manage their time effectively and they don't get caught up in the noise.

9. They are passionate and curious of the world around them. They are lifelong learners.

Step One: Self-Confidence

If you believe that by asking for introductions you will diminish your brand, or that it somehow makes you come across desperate, all I can do is urge you to reconsider your position. Is your hesitancy to ask for introductions truly for those reasons, or is it more of a matter of feeling shy and uncomfortable at the thought of doing it? If so, ask yourself whether you have the desire to grow your business, the vision, and the model to offer success to potential clients. If the answer is yes, you can't provide those services by waiting for clients to come to you. If you have confidence in your abilities, it should not be hard to ask for an introduction. With a healthy sense of confidence, it doesn't matter as much when you get rejected—because there will be rejection—it matters more that you have built the appropriate mental momentum that nothing gets in the way. Plus, top advisors don't take rejection personally.

Just as I used to talk to myself before a football game, I do so now before I go on stage for a presentation as a way to build up my confidence. Everything starts and ends with confidence. In our business we become masters of hiding and compartmentalizing our feelings; therefore, it is harder to notice when someone lacks confidence. We don't ask for introductions because we lack confidence, not because it's hard work. It's a simple concept, but it's not always easy to execute. You just have to embrace the motto, "Sometimes you win; sometimes you lose." But if you don't play the game, I guarantee you will never win.

Step Two: Get Your House in Order

Introductions happen naturally when your house is in order, when you have the right people in the right roles delivering a fantastic client experience. This creates loyal and happy clients. In turn, you feel comfortable asking these clients for introductions and, even better, they are more likely to make an introduction without asking. How do you know your clients are happy? The most obvious way is when they transfer more assets to you. People vote with their feet.

But we also can't operate under the old adage, "No news is good news." We can't rest on our laurels and assume that because a client hasn't expressed dissatisfaction they are happy with your services. It's essential to ask your clients at least once a year how you can better serve them. You want to know what you're doing right, what you're doing wrong, and what you and your team can do better. Most people use a one-page survey, and that can have some benefit, but I recommend a face-to-face meeting with your best clients so that you can ask them directly. Have a meaningful conversation and take notes. You need to make sure that your clients value your services before you just start asking for introductions. Nothing could be worse than asking a client to make an introduction only to be told no because the client hasn't been happy with what you've been doing and is considering changing advisors.

Success breeds more success. In other words, stack the deck in your favor right out of the gate. The foundation is simple: you don't have the right to ask for anything unless you have made enough emotional deposits and you're meeting or exceeding the client's expectations. Ultimately, only a small percentage of your clients will go out of their way to introduce you to their friends and family unsolicited. Most clients will not initiate an introduction for a number of reasons:

- The client may think you're too busy to take on more clients.
- Clients may think if they make an introduction, they will lose their privacy.
- The client may not know how to properly introduce you and all the services you provide.

Research I have seen over the last 30 years indicates that 80 percent of clients are never asked for an introduction. They also go on to say that if they were asked, 77 percent would give one. A great way to start getting your business on the right track is to create a client advisory board, made up of 8 to 10 clients who meet over dinner twice a year. Their job is to provide open feedback on ways to improve your services.

Step Three: Reciprocity

Reciprocity has been around since the beginning of time, yet people in our business can't seem to employ it effectively in the interest of creating the best outcome for you and the client. Every deal needs to be a win-win and the person with the best leverage has the upper hand. In the end, I want my client to say, "You are irreplaceable." I want clients to be so happy with our relationship that when I do ask for an introduction, it will not feel like I'm "asking," but rather I'm "offering." That's a big difference. Asking can come across like it's only a deal for you and that it's all about you and the growth of your business. When you have the mindset that you're offering to help one of their friends, it feels different. If you believe in your value so strongly, you naturally offer your services because you believe others will be in better hands by working with you.

Teach your clients how to introduce you. They are busy and they don't need another thing to do, so make it easy for them. Once you know they are willing to introduce you, give them a very short one-pager that tells them:

- Who you are
- What you do
- What makes you different

Plant the seed from the very start, at the initial discovery meeting. Part of that meeting should include time for you to share how you built the business and how your business continues to grow. It can end with a statement about always being grateful for referrals. For example, you might say, "Robert and Mary, it's been a pleasure meeting you today and we feel confident that we can meet your expectations.

Our goal, however, is to exceed your expectations because our business is built on referrals. We always welcome an introduction if our services meet and exceed your expectations, and our goal is to do that every day, it's not to push product."

Of course, say it in your own way, but stating something like this does a few key things. First, it lets clients know that you and your team are motivated to do a great job for them because that's how your business grows; second, you're informing the client that you encourage and appreciate an introduction; and third, you are being completely transparent about your business. Remember, it only feels like begging if you're not adding value to the client's experience. In return, when you feel confident that you're delivering an outstanding client experience, you feel like a champion.

Step Four: Motivation

Why would someone go out of her way to help you? Well, maybe your client is going out of her way to help a friend. The client is convinced that her friend would be better off in your hands or she is trying to do a favor for someone she cares about. It's your job to understand and get into your client's head to see what motivates them. Needs and recognition can be a powerful motivator. If someone makes an introduction, you had better make a really big deal of it. Most people will call the client and say thank you. That's not a big deal. It's the very least you can do. It's important to make the client who made the introduction feel like a super VIP:

1. Absolutely call and say thank you. And remind the client again that you honor privacy and never discuss other people's matters with anyone.

2. Send the client a small gift (under $30) of thanks with a handwritten note.
3. Take the client out to lunch or dinner.
4. Thank the client again a few weeks or months later and tell him or her how much you appreciated the introduction and how much you enjoy working with the new clients.
5. Never discuss the confidentiality with one client to another.

How to Ask for Introductions

How did you learn to ride a bike? It took practice and persistence most likely. Learn how to ask for introductions by starting to ask for introductions. It may feel awkward in the beginning and you may hear "no," but the more you ask, the more you learn, the better you get, and the more yeses you begin to hear. Finessing the way you ask takes practice. If you do it like most—wing it—it shows. Develop a style that speaks to your brand. Remember, it's how you frame the request. Choose your words carefully. But, most importantly, keep it simple. Being yourself is key. Be transparent.

"John, you told me how much you enjoy working with our team and how you are very satisfied with the level of services. Do you still feel that way?" Once John responds with "Yes," you continue. "First, I want to say thank you for placing your trust in us. It's a pleasure working with you and we all appreciate your business. We know we have to earn your trust every day. The reason I asked the first question is because I would like to continue to grow my business with more people like you. Can I help you think of some people who may want a second opinion about their portfolio?"

In the end, growing your business with a focus on introductions is the most efficient and effective tool in your box.

Developing Advocates

In addition to becoming a trusted advisor to your clients, it's beneficial to cultivate a special group of clients for yourself, ones I call *advocates*. Developing advocates is based on the approach that it is better to have fewer accounts of higher quality with more assets than a large number of lower quality accounts with fewer assets. About one hundred relationships is the right number for many advisors.

Client advocates are ones who trust and believe strongly enough in you that they go out of their way to refer business to you. They can give you access to a network of people with significant assets to invest.

Obviously, developing advocates means building relationships. Those relationships have to be genuine, which is not so easy because it takes time. These clients have to genuinely like you and you have to genuinely like them. There has to be chemistry and trust. You can find people who want to help you grow your business, but only if they truly value what you are all about—your whole makeup. At some point, it becomes hard to separate advocates from friends.

Your baseline for developing advocates is making sure you are serving them to the best of your ability and that you are competent in their eyes. While you should survey all your clients, your advocate development campaign will be based on selecting good clients whose opinions and judgment you respect.

The second part of the process is more personal: spending quality time with clients outside the office and getting to know them on a more personal level. I do it by going to dinner, to a sporting event, and so forth.

Some clients will turn into advocates on their own, without prodding. With others, you have to ask. "Bob, I know you have placed trust in our team to manage all of your wealth management needs. That level of trust means a lot to me. You're an influential person with friends who could probably use our services and if there's any way you could help, I would appreciate it."

Since advocates are clients, you must continue to maintain high levels of communication with them. Ask them to be candid with you: "If you think I'm doing something that's not consistent with what I'm trying to achieve, I would hope that you would tell me—not just when I ask, but any time. Pick up the phone and let me know, 'Your sales assistant has dropped the ball,' or 'Your firm is doing something I don't like.'" Five to ten advocates with major spheres of influence can have a major impact on your business.

Community Engagement and Networking

Community involvement can be another form of networking—a very effective one—but it has to be done even more unselfishly than networking as community service and charity work is about doing something from the heart, for the good of your community.

I believe many people don't get involved because the world's problems seem too big for a single person to have an effect. You don't have to change the world; you only have to change one person as the saying goes. Try devoting four or five hours a week to charity. Find something you enjoy and that allows you to make a difference. It will enrich your life more than any material object can.

It's also an opportunity to make business contacts, although it's the least important reason to do it. If you volunteer at a nonprofit for your own business purposes, it won't happen and you will waste your time. Think with your heart when you are thinking about an organization you might want to be involved with. Over time, you will find yourself developing long-term win–win relationships with other volunteers. You will also find yourself surrounded by good people—people who actually do good as opposed to people who just talk about doing good.

You can get involved with cultural organizations, fundraising activities, the Chamber of Commerce, athletic associations, colleges, your local high school, homeowners' associations, sporting events, art shows, hospitals, and more. The list is endless. You will learn how other people live, experience new environments, and pick up useful new skills. Depending on the organization to which you offer your time, even some of your professional skills may be useful to the organization. Ultimately, you will gain new insights into yourself, which only increases your self-awareness.

In terms of making community involvement work for your business, the key is to get active and be visible immediately. While not everyone in each area of exposure is a prospect, you can quickly build a sphere of influence that can be expanded over time.

As I've said before, you can't hide your character, so it is important to get involved for the right reasons. Give back without looking for paybacks.

Percentage Willing to Refer by Age Group

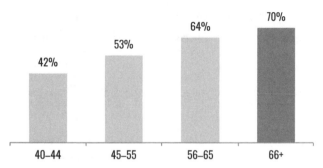

Source: McKinsey

Percentage Willing to Refer by Affluence

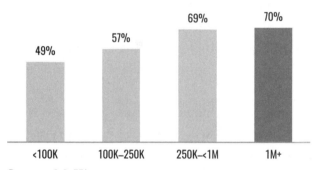

Source: McKinsey

Present a Successful Seminar

Leading or presenting in professional seminars can be an effective way to attract clients and grow your business. But, it takes a lot of hard work, a solid process, and you can't just do one and done. Hold a seminar once every month and focus on quality of attendees, not quantity. Having 20 people attend is fine if they know that for them to be a client they need at least $1 million of investable assets. Also, if public speaking is not your strength, bring in an outside speaker. Think about a partnership with an accounting firm or a group that gets together already and you become a guest speaker. I talked about my tips on public speaking in Part One of the book. Here are my tips for creating a successful seminar.

1. Make sure your presentation works before you use it on a crowd. Ask a friend—one who will be honest with you—to critique you.
2. Rehearsing is very important. Recite your entire presentation at least three times before the day of the seminar. Don't wing it.
3. Carefully target your invitations.
4. Make the seminar short, direct, and easy to understand.
5. Remember that it's not just what you say, it's how you say it. (Be a crowd pleaser.) If you speak technical industry jargon in a monotone voice, your prospects will drift away.
6. The most important thing is to connect with the audience. Pick out individuals and make eye contact with them for three to four seconds at a time. Make sure to do this for every person in attendance.
7. Get immediate feedback by asking attendees to fill out a confidential questionnaire. The only way to get better is to ask how you did!
8. Follow up. Send out notes thanking them for attending and invite them to call you if they have any questions or want to discuss their situations. Put them on your mailing list for newsletters.

If you are truly committed to business development, focus on buying assets. Buying a book can take a long time to find the right fit and valuation.

Social Media

Although the financial industry has been late to adopt it, the value of social media is finally starting to sink in. From RIA firms to the larger wirehouses, financial institutions are looking to harness the power of social media now more than ever. They are becoming more and more comfortable with the regulations and starting to really get the concept of social media and how it can be used for business.

Courtney McQuade is an expert in financial technology and social media, with a specific focus on marketing and sales strategy. Over the past 18 years, she has worked at startups, hedge funds, private equity firms, and several of Wall Street's largest banks. I met Courtney in New York City about 15 years ago while we were both working at Prudential Securities. We reconnected a few years ago on—where else—LinkedIn. I recently caught up with her and asked about some of the trends she's seeing and why it's so important for advisors to include social media in their strategy.

Rick: Social media, to a lot of people, still seems like just a platform for fun. How can it actually tie into an advisor's business strategy?

Courtney: That's a very common question I get, Rick. You've heard the old cliché, "life is sales." You could be an amazing attorney, personal trainer, and so on, but if you don't know how to market yourself, to *sell* yourself, no one is ever going to know how good you are and want your services. Social media is the perfect place to prove yourself as a thought leader in your industry. Post content your clients and prospects want to know about, want to learn, breaking down the latest news in the market in a way they can easily digest and understand. Show that you have a real finger on the pulse of what's happening and how it applies it to their needs.

In a joint study by Cognet Research and LinkedIn, "Nearly two in five of the mass affluent use social media for discovery or consideration of financial companies, products, policies, or accounts (36%); among mass affluent who use social media for both purposes, nearly two in three (63%) take action as a result of what they learn."

It's also the perfect platform to build your personal brand and connect with people; not just to show that you know what you're doing, but to show the kind of person you are, what interests you have, humanizing yourself. I always tell my clients, "People like to do business with people, not companies—show them who you are as a person." If you like to cook, travel, sew, volunteer, whatever you're passionate about, share some of this on social media. Your clients and potential clients will enjoy seeing the human side of you—the mother, the father, the artist, the philanthropist, someone who might have something in common with them. Social media is the perfect place to form bonds with clients and prospects.

Rick: Quite a few advisors seem to feel uncomfortable posting things about themselves, even if it's purely professional; is this something you see as well?

Courtney: For sure. Different generations have different feelings related to posting things about themselves on social media—some tend to feel like it's bragging and I totally understand that. To the millennial generation it's normal to post your life experiences and/or knowledge online, to share your personal thoughts and feelings. But to the baby boomer generation, and even the generations in between, it might feel weird, awkward, invasive, or like bragging.

But we now live in an information age. One thing I think we all can agree on is that people now do all their research online. (Although I still enjoy a paper copy of *Barron's* in my hands on Sundays.) It can definitely take some getting used to, so I always tell my advisors to start small with just one or two LinkedIn posts a week, to start getting comfortable with it. Follow other companies and thought leaders in our industry on LinkedIn and try to incorporate just 10 to 15 minutes a day, reading through your Linked-In Home feed, the same way you'd read through the *Wall Street Journal* or Bloomberg newsfeed.

A lot of advisors already are getting comfortable with it. An internal study done last year at Morgan Stanley showed that 46% of its advisors who use social media used it to connect with their clients' children and grandchildren. And 57% reported bringing in new assets through their social media engagement.

Rick: So, basically, if an advisor is not currently using LinkedIn, he might be losing out to the advisors who are.

Courtney: That's exactly right, Rick. Every day you're not active on LinkedIn is a missed opportunity to connect with prospects, reinforce your value to clients, and build your credibility as a forward-looking investment expert. You may also be losing mindshare to competitors who have invested the time and thought that it takes to establish a strong social media presence. Social media is now one of the leading forms of communication. It is how we connect with one another, and it is how we research the companies we are considering doing business with. No longer is a company's website enough to gain credibility; people want to see what advisors have to say and how much they know. Now, businesses are translating this knowledge through social media.

Not to mention, by default, a LinkedIn profile is your professional online identity. If a potential client Googles you, it will most likely be their first stop to learn more about you.

Rick: LinkedIn seems like the obvious platform all advisors should be using, but what about Facebook?

Courtney: I hear a lot of advisors now talking about taking a "holistic approach" to investment planning with their clients, which means not just taking their net worth and allocating it into the appropriate investment vehicles; it means taking into account their lifestyle, their passions, specific family dynamics, and more. A few years ago, Facebook would not have been recommended as a good business platform for our industry. But now advisors are starting to connect with their clients through Facebook and although they may not be posting industry knowledge or opinions on the platform, they are using it to keep that personal relationship by sharing family photos and major life events. And in turn they can see when their clients are posting vacation photos, retirement party photos, and other life events. They can use Facebook as talking points in client meetings and/or as indicators for the time to contact their clients.

Now, as an advisor, if you do choose to use your personal Facebook to connect with clients, because historically it has been so very personal, you might want to tone down some of your posts and potentially go back in your Timeline and clean up a little, depending on your past posting style.

> "Success consists of going from failure to failure without loss of enthusiasm."
>
> —*Winston Churchill*

Think Like an Owner and Invest in Your Business

Successful advisors believe so strongly in their own future that they are willing to ante up now. They know every dollar put back into their business will produce sustainable growth in the future. This principle doesn't just apply to larger practices with staffs of 10 or more, but to a solo practitioner who recognizes that having his or her own assistant, for instance, would create tremendous advantages. This is about taking personal responsibility for the rate of growth one chooses and then making it happen. Proven strategies of investing back into the business are the following; human capital, technology, business development, marketing, or buying assets.

Investing back into the business means different things to different advisors. It could mean a comprehensive targeted marketing campaign or buying another wealth manager's book of business. If you aren't reinvesting in your business, then you are underestimating, undervaluing, and underrating your business, your team, your firm, and, of course, yourself. Are you a growth stock? Would you invest in your stock?

Of course, investing back into your business for the wirehouse advisor will come with a different set of priorities than those for the RIA advisor. For the RIA, it's about creating scale; for many, it's breaking the $1 billion mark while for others it's $10 billion. Therefore, investing back into the business is all based on where you are now. The larger RIAs or IBDs focus on providing the best technology possible and they focus on acquisitions, marketing, and the right level of client support to achieve an outstanding client experience. Business development is one area where allocation of resources will be paramount.

Chapter 15

Exceptional Client Experience

"Quality is never an accident; it is always the result of high intention, sincere effort, intelligent direction and skillful execution; it represents the wise choice of many alternatives."

—*William A. Foster*

As I discussed in Chapter 3, we can't have a great client experience without an outstanding culture. Because there are more than 300,000 advisors in the United States alone and most use similar products and business platforms, it's vital to set yourself apart. Separating your team from the overcrowded army of advisors starts with delivering excellence. The best news is the fact that clients value a great client experience, and providing that is completely in your control. Great service has a well-defined vision, strategy, and process. The future will demand you segment your clients and provide the appropriate level of service for each group of clients. Platinum clients and silver clients can't receive the same level of attention and service. Everyone is committed and focused on getting the little things right. Let me say this differently: people get the big things right, but what separates you from the rest is getting the little things right—paying attention to the smallest details. Because if you can't get the small details right, you will be just like everyone else. In order to create a great client experience you need to leverage technology and have a well-defined process working in collaboration with digital labor. It allows you as the advisor to establish the emotional connection with your client.

A Successful Collaboration

Ask Yourself:
- Do I do more listening than talking?
- Does everyone on the team understand what it means to deliver exceptional service?
- Does everyone on the team understand that he or she has a job because of the client?
- Does everybody understand how much time and energy goes into acquiring a relationship but that it takes only seconds to lose one?
- Does the team get together once a week to adjust the service model and improve the experience by discussing specific clients?
- Do I ask great questions?
- Am I focused on building long-term relationships?
- Am I selling the next SMA or the next model portfolio, or trying to select the next growth stock?
- Am I always putting my clients' interests first by truly listening to what's important to them?

Across the industry, there is a lack of consistency in the service model for the high-net-worth client. Since your service offering is the most controllable part of your business, you can gain substantial market share with a tight and consistent service model that delivers an exceptional client experience every time. The number one reason clients switch advisors is because of service-relationship issues, not because of investment performance. Having a healthy pipeline of potential clients is key. Staying connected with these prospects by sending them information or looking for ways to build the relationship will prove beneficial over time because in some cases the existing client–advisor

Percentage of Clients, by Age Group, Who Switched Advisors

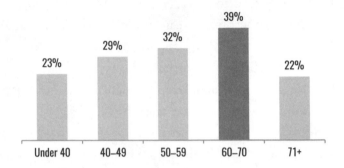

When Do Clients Switch Advisors?

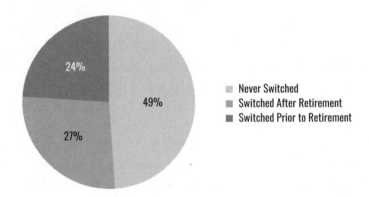

relationship breaks down. As the above charts show, clients do switch firms, and if they have a place to go because you have been dripping useful information on them, they are more likely to move faster.

At the end of the day, it is all about the client experience, which starts with the right culture and hiring the right people. We have to make it easy for clients to do business with us and it is in this area that we as an industry most need to improve. Advisors need to be their clients' biggest advocates and clear the path for them, providing solutions that the client will value, not ones that you or your firm value.

Little Things Make a Big Difference: The Fundamentals Matter a Great Deal

Offering a well-defined service model entails a clear understanding of client goals, a descriptive financial plan, regular client contact, and periodic portfolio reviews. After an in-depth discovery meeting, presenting the client with a proposal and an investment policy statement sets clear expectations and lays the foundation for you to deliver exceptional service. Interestingly enough, little things mean a lot in these endeavors. Answering phone calls before three rings, responding to emails in a timely fashion (within a few hours for your platinum clients), having the receptionist greet clients enthusiastically and by name, and, of course, providing clients with extras are generally greatly appreciated. I call this "off-core" client services, meaning you do something your client does not expect from you. Therefore, if you want to impress them, focus on what is off-core. Look for opportunities to leave lasting impressions. A great client experience is all about expectations and client expectations are on the rise.

The most important meeting by far is the discovery meeting, which I'll discuss in more detail in the next chapter. The discovery meeting is the time when you must not only show that you're someone who is competent but also someone they can fully trust. It requires transparency and authenticity to differentiate you from the rest. As an advisor, I started every meeting with the end in mind, in other words what I hoped to accomplish in the meeting. With all my networking and interactions today, I still see people who are not fully authentic or vulnerable. The same holds true for some advisors during a client meeting. The following questions are not only important during the discovery meeting but also meant to help you understand the prospect in order to exceed expectations and customize a service model that they will value.

Ask the prospect:
- What is important to you over the next five years?
- What do you worry about most?
- In choosing a firm, what are two things that matter most?
- What are you passionate about?
- What is your vision for these assets?
- How would you describe great service?
- How often would you like to meet?
- What's generally the best time for us to get together?
- In terms of communication, what's your preference, text, email, or phone call?

A typical investment generalist provides an initial predetermined financial plan and only contacts the client when transactions are the topic of discussion. Due to the large number of clients, he or she is generally unable to provide the time needed for monthly calls and periodic reviews. For a wealth manager, it is these points of contact that truly build the relationship. It's the off-core services that will make you stand out. It's the little things, the little details—a black car to pick them up; a high-end leather document holder; using real china when you offer a cup of coffee—they do not expect and yet will wow them. Do you already do things such as this? What else can you do? Ask yourself and your clients on a regular basis, "What can we do to stand out from everyone in the business claiming the same services?" You are not in the volume business; it's about the quality of these relationships and therefore everyone should have antennas up all the time to look for opportunity to leave a lasting impression. When someone on the team does go out of her way to impress a client, don't keep it a secret.

You can't provide great service without an outstanding sales assistant; it's impossible without the right support. It's one of the biggest opportunities I see to providing outstanding client service. And it's also the biggest mistake advisors make, not investing in their own business. First, hire the right people for the right role. If you hire someone who will be talking to clients on a daily basis, he'd better like working with people and have great interpersonal skills. Are his soft skills up to date? Are they going to new training on a regular basis? Attracting, developing, and retaining talented support staff is a must and it's one of the biggest differences between an elite team and everyone else. Most importantly, as I discussed in Chapter 3, the person in the assistant role must feel respected and valued. It's amazing to me why some teams don't invest in having their own assistant if they can afford it. I think of this group of professionals as the glue to the overarching relationship. Go out of your way to show gratitude, say thank you, send handwritten notes, and celebrate their special occasions. The best way to create the right behavior is

Exceptional Client Experience

Authentic

Efficient

Knowledgeable

Empathetic

Empowered

to align incentive to percentage of business and growth, client retention, and client loyalty.

> "Human greatness does not lie in wealth or power, but in character and goodness. People are just people, and all people have faults and shortcomings, but all of us are born with a basic goodness."
>
> —*Anne Frank*

The Best Gift Is Client Feedback

Requesting feedback from your clients is a good way to gauge whether they are happy with your services. You might send a note such as the following:

Dear ___:

I would like to take this moment to thank you for giving us the opportunity to help you achieve your financial goals.

From time to time, I would like to check in with you to ensure that you are receiving the level of service you expect and deserve. I would appreciate you taking a few moments to provide me with feedback on areas we can improve upon.

Please be candid in your responses and feel free to discuss any topics that are not in the survey. I'd like to thank you in advance for taking the time to help me determine ways in which we can better serve you.

Very truly yours,_____

Asking for feedback is key, but I would use good judgment about which clients you choose to send the survey to. For example, you probably shouldn't send a request for feedback via email to your top 25 clients. You should schedule a face-to-face meeting with these clients to demonstrate how much you value their time and opinion. Frankly, they might find it insulting to receive a request for feedback via email as it could be interpreted as an impersonal gesture.

Listen to Your Clients on a Regular Basis

Those closest to the client have all the power. It's not the person in the C-suite and it's not the person who sees a client once a year. It's the advisor who truly understands the clients' needs. The best advisors ask, "How am I doing?" or "What can we do better?" on a regular basis. Know your clients. If you send a survey to your best clients whom you have worked with for 10 years, you are insulting them. They need and expect a more personal touch. Take them out to lunch and have a one-on-one conversation. Create a diverse group of smart people who can serve as advisors to you and your business. Create a safe environment for people to speak their minds in terms of what you and your firm could do differently to increase the overall client experience. Listening means many things to the client. One, this advisor cares. Two, this advisor wants to improve the service. Three, this advisor is open to suggestions. Show respect by asking for their opinion. It's a good way to evaluate how you're doing, where you are, and what adjustments you need to make. So get into the habit of asking for feedback on a regular basis. As I said earlier, time is very precious to the high-net-worth individual; therefore keep the asking simple. When these clients come to the office for a review, send them an email simply asking one question about the experience. For example, on a scale of one to five, how would you rate your experience? It would be productive to know in real time how they feel about the experience. But if you send them an email that takes 20 seconds, they may do it. If it was a poor experience, of course you will follow up immediately and find out why.

Communication and Connections

The key to communicating and connecting with clients is getting into their heads to understand what is important to them. There are a number of keywords and phrases that make people feel good and influence their thought. I like to use "You can count on me." (And again, don't say anything you don't truly mean. Authenticity only makes statements such as this truthful.)

Some of the keywords that tend to resonate with clients include:

- safe(ty)
- solid(ity)
- dependable(ity)
- reliable(ity)
- substantial
- consistent(cy)
- preserve
- protect
- conserve
- anchor
- support
- prudent
- wise
- reasonable
- grow
- enrich
- enhance
- flexible

In addition to understanding what language might appeal to clients, ensure everyone on your team is trained on and subscribes to the same operating philosophy: "The client doesn't need us; we need them." Implement processes such as team meetings the day before a client meeting so everyone is up to date, the client's expectations are understood, and the meeting's goals are clear.

Communication creates the infrastructure for building an ongoing relationship. Do you have a strategy in place that ensures proactive contact with the right clients at the right time? Do you reach out to them even more during market downturns? The media may create unnecessary anxiety that makes investors increasingly concerned, especially when markets are volatile. How are you going to mitigate these fears before they become entrenched?

Beware of information overload as it can create even more confusion and hence a greater need for interpretation and perspective by a trusted, competent advisor. Money can make people very emotional, especially during market volatility. A trusted advisor keeps a client on course and away from panic.

Eliminate Red Tape

Many high-net-worth clients are successful in their own right and fully understand how to run a prosperous business. They don't want to hear about bureaucratic processes within your organization that bog them down in red tape, or that bog you down, preventing them from receiving the information they want. Therefore, it is always best to under-promise and over-deliver. If and when breakdowns in service quality do occur, take full responsibility immediately and put a predetermined recovery or reward system into action, such as a handwritten note, personal phone call, or face-to-face meeting. Most importantly, don't be a victim and engage in the blame game.

> "I want you to listen to what your conscience commands you to do and go on to carry it out to the best of your knowledge. Then you will live to see that in the long run—in the long run, I say!—success will follow you precisely because you had forgotten to think of it."
>
> —*Victor E. Frankl*

Seize every opportunity to build the client relationship. Begin with how you build and deliver your clients' plans. Do not mail it. Present it in person. It is an excellent opportunity to build and deepen the relationship.

Advisors must work collaboratively with the client who wishes to maintain control of his or her financial affairs in order to arrive at decisions that are in keeping with the client's short-term, intermediate-term, and long-term goals. Keep the client informed on a regular basis, systematically review portfolios, and provide timely updates.

A high-quality client service model involves anticipating opportunities that will not only help you make a difference in the client experience, but will also help you cater to these high-net-worth individuals even before they communicate their needs. Opportunities may present themselves in the form of complaints. Likewise, don't assume that no news is good news. Always ask your clients the simplest questions on a regular basis, such as: "How are we doing?" and "What can I do to make our interactions even more beneficial for you?"

Client Appreciation Events

Lunches, dinners, and holiday parties—these settings provide multiple opportunities to build relationships by letting clients see you as a person, showing your appreciation for their business, and sharing new information in a relaxed, low-key setting.

Invite your top 50 clients and ask them to bring friends. Do a full-blown dinner that shows you appreciate their business. You will probably get 20 to 25 attendees, but that is all right.

Take all your "A" clients out to lunch during the holidays. Invite each to bring a friend. Bring along a camera (or hire a photographer) and share the pictures with them at your next meeting (email photos and a note to those who can't attend). It is expensive, but worth it. The pictures also serve as an icebreaker. People like to see themselves and talk about the great time they had the previous year. Client appreciation events are about showing your appreciation and cultivating your relationship. If these types of events are not your style, think of other creative ways to engage with your best clients. It may be a sporting event, a cooking class, a yoga class, or an art show. It's about how creative you like to get.

Quarterly and Annual Client Reviews

One of the best opportunities advisors have to demonstrate an exceptional client experience is during the quarterly and annual reviews. These meetings are the cornerstones to successful client communication. During the meeting, you may have several opportunities to enforce client retention (increasing wallet share), to build greater loyalty, or perhaps to ask for an introduction. Depending on how you segment your clients, most should have a quarterly review. A quarterly review could occur via phone, but make sure your clients have had a chance to review their quarterly report before the phone call. Of course, face-to-face meetings are always best because you tend to learn a great deal more about changes in your clients' lives. For your very best clients, you may want to set up monthly reviews. Ask your top clients what they prefer if you don't know. For other clients, an annual review is sufficient.

For each review meeting, you should provide a standard short report with a summary on the first page. Do your homework, because if you don't and just try to wing it, the client will know. The client will also know if you rush the process because you feel the client doesn't deserve this level of service. Simple communication about clients' expectations for the reviews can help you plan for the meetings properly. How much time should you spend preparing for the review? As you know, it depends on the size of the relationship; for some it could be as short as 30 minutes and for other clients as much as two hours or longer. It depends on the size and complexity of the relationship.

These reviews should discuss the following topics/questions:

- What's changed in your life since our last review? Have you experienced any major life events?
- How am I doing? Is our portfolio asset allocation still right for you in this market environment? Do we need to make any changes?
- Gains/losses.
- Share your market perspective with your clients. Provide any explanation or justification for why they

should maintain a certain percentage of assets in cash, equity, or fixed income, and so on.

- Discuss wealth management issues, including:
  - Estate planning
  - Retirement
  - Philanthropic and charitable giving
  - Asset titling
  - Liabilities
  - Cash flow
  - Insurance
  - Income taxes
  - Spending

Use these meetings as opportunities to ask if your service level is meeting your client's expectations. High-net-worth clients tend to have high expectations, but when you exceed those expectations, they become your fans. About 90 percent of "highly satisfied" clients are likely to make referrals while only 15 percent of "moderately satisfied" clients would give you a referral. Therefore, it pays to know precisely how your clients feel about your service and your team.

Lastly, one of the best gifts a client can give you is feedback. Positive or negative feedback is critical to the client experience. However, if you don't ask on a regular basis, you are operating in the dark. And it's too late if your client has already begun to think about moving his accounts. I like to end most meetings—not just review meetings—with the question, "Is there anything I can do for you?" This question shows your clients you are focused on them, shows you're a giver, and shows that you have the influence to make things happen.

Chapter 16

Discovery Meeting

"Nature gave us one tongue and two ears so we could hear twice as much as we speak."

—*Epictetus*

If we stop and think about it for a second, the discovery meeting is by far the most important client meeting. It lays the foundation for the relationship, creates expectations, and is the first step in forming a deep understanding of a client's objectives. What I have come to realize is that too often this process is rushed, creating a multitude of missed opportunities to truly understand the dreams of this prospect. We all want to gain trust immediately. And this first meeting is all about gaining trust. Without trust, you will not move forward. The quickest way to gain trust is to compress time. And you do that by being fully transparent, and asking compelling questions. You put everything on the table. You avoid coming across as a robot; you're human, you've made mistakes, and you acknowledge that you don't know it all. In short, if you want your clients to open up, you must open up first.

Avoid judgment. Create a safe environment for people to open up without judgment or sarcasm. Additionally, think of the discovery phase as a never-ending process. The team can always learn something new about the client. The relationship between an investor and his or her money is complex, private, and, in many countries around the world, completely secret. The best advisors break down barriers in their clients' minds and persuade them to express their dreams and fears while also encouraging a deeper level of trust in sharing what money really means to them.

In Chapter 1, I discussed how communication is the most important tool we have in creating strong trusting relationships with clients and colleagues. Successful advisors devote a lot of time to continuously improving this important skill set. The best communicators say more with fewer words, are active listeners, and ask thought-provoking questions. Let's face it—people in general have an attention span of two or three minutes. I usually make the assumption that people are not listening; therefore, I am reminded to work hard to make sure my point is getting through. For me, one of the biggest factors in identifying whether someone is trustworthy is their ability to listen. In other words, is a person who listens more and talks less more trustworthy? If you think about it, it makes sense. Sometimes those who talk a lot seem like they are trying to sell something, whether it be an idea, point of view, product, or something else. The following discovery diagram should serve as a guide to help you stay focused on the discovery process.

Discovery Diagram

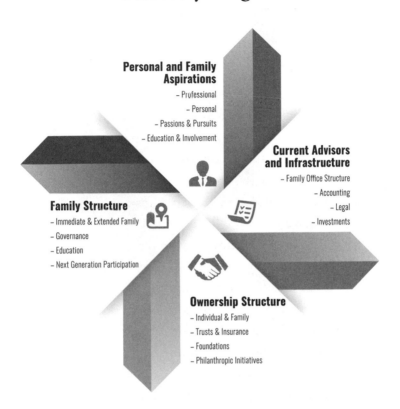

If the ability to communicate effectively is a successful advisor's most important tool, listening is the most significant component and, for many people, least developed part of communication. Truly listening takes energy, empathy, maturity, and a high level of emotional intelligence. During the discovery meeting you and your team should be talking 20 percent of the time and listening the other 80 percent. This is not the meeting to showcase your platform and your investment philosophy. That happens in the second meeting. Yes, you are also trying to impress the prospect on what you can do for them, but don't go overboard; a vendor does that, not a true professional wealth manager.

As I mentioned in Part One of the book, ancient Greek philosophers can teach us a lot about communication. From Aristotle we learn that if you want to persuade someone, whether it's your audience or your clients, you need to first show your character (ethos); second, reveal your emotions to make a personal connection (pathos); and third, prove your logic (logos).

Your ethos is defined by how credible and trustworthy you are. Demonstrating one's ethos through action is more powerful than simply talking about one's character.

Pathos provides the emotional connection, sharing your authentic self. When you reveal something personal about yourself or share your dreams, hopes, aspirations, or worries, generally the client will open up as well. Relationships are shared experiences. As robo-advisors begin to play a greater role in our industry, our emotional connections can make a big difference in our client relationships.

Our logos is the part of ourselves focused on logic, data, and process. For example, we use our logos when we present evidence of historical returns to make a point about investment performance.

This three-pronged model works. In fact, it's stood the test of time for over 2,300 years. The best advisors know how to weave ethos, pathos, and logos into their conversations. A team that engages all three components in their client conversations can be very powerful because one person can be the relationship builder while the others can execute the technical aspects of wealth management.

Going Deeper Than "Cocktail Talk": Intuitive Listening

Our culture loves conversation that doesn't mean anything. Most often at a cocktail party, all you hear is a loud buzz. Most of this conversation doesn't amount to anything. People are trying to outdo or impress others, and most of it is superficial. The people attending the party aren't necessarily shallow, but they are following the unspoken rules of what a cocktail party is supposed to be. More often than not you leave with a big headache and the need for aspirin.

But you don't have to get involved in meaningless cocktail conversation with clients or coworkers. You can engender trust by giving people insights into who you are. Try being yourself: be open, vulnerable, and deep. If you have the courage to let people see the real you, they will start to trust you. Have the courage to care, be warm, be emotional (but not overly emotional) and make people feel special.

Deep down most people want to deal with *real* people. Being real means admitting your failures as well as your successes. Being real also means sharing sad moments alongside the happy ones. You cannot fake it. Your body language, eyes, and voice tell your story.

Emotional Intelligence Matters

Although logic and discipline are critical to being an advisor, they can sometimes get in the way when you don't use the other side of your brain to connect with clients on a more emotional level. Clients care a great deal about the numbers. But it is what the numbers mean in terms of their overall goals, life, and future that ultimately matters

to the clients. That means the presentation is often as important as, if not more important than, content. To put it more
simply: how you say something is just as important as what
you're saying.

Use Your Soft Skills

One of the greatest distinctions between leaders and managers as well as high-performing advisors versus average
advisors is the ability of leaders to inspire people on a consistent basis. You can't inspire others if you are not inspired
yourself and you cannot inspire yourself if you do not
invest time and effort into developing your emotional
intelligence.

Research indicates that emotional intelligence is what
distinguishes outstanding performers from average ones.
The best advisors know how to ask emotionally based
questions. The perception may be that advisors are good
at talking, but the best advisors appear to ask high-quality
questions derived from being an attentive, active listener.
These advisors understand that a connection with a client
starts as a meeting of the hearts, before becoming a meeting
of the minds.

Psychological research also suggests that advisors with a
high level of emotional intelligence are likable, trustworthy,
and competent. They have a great ability to take complex
information and explain it in a compelling and simplified
manner. They are great storytellers and that makes them
effective communicators. People remember stories and
metaphors much more intensely than the seventh point on

slide #47 of a PowerPoint presentation. Such emotional intelligence is vital to having a successful discovery meeting.

Compelling Questions Make a Difference

A key part of a discovery meeting is asking questions that allow your clients to tell you their story—not the story you want to hear, but the story that's important to them, that will help you understand what you need to do to help them succeed. You elicit this story with personal, open-ended questions:

- You've been very successful. What are you most proud of?
- What are you hoping to accomplish over the next 5 to 10 years?
- How would you describe a comfortable retirement?
- How do you spend your free time? What are you passionate about?
- Do you think you will be responsible for one of your parents or in-laws at some point in the future?
- How much longer do you believe you will work?
- From a financial point of view, what concerns you most?
- How would you describe a reasonable return based on your risk tolerance?
- Is there anything we discussed that needs to be clarified?

Clearly, these are not questions that center around value versus growth styles, or that analyze different pie charts or asset allocations. Those communications are important and will eventually happen, but the emotional component of the relationship helps build a meaningful dialogue that can allow you to weather volatile markets, as well as helping your clients achieve their important goals.

Successful advisors work hard to understand their clients from the beginning of the relationship. Waiting until the market is down 20 percent may be a painful lesson. Beginning that process from the very beginning and building it steadily and constantly over the long term makes having those hard conversations, when they come, easier.

Milestones Matter

There are certain defining moments that occur in building and deepening every client relationship and you must be acutely aware of these moments and seize the opportunities that they represent. If you are an active, intuitive listener with an organized business and stay connected with the client's changing life, you can build a meaningful rapport that endures over many years.

Life-changing events for a client can include those that are business-related (promotions, relocations, reorganizations), family-related (births, deaths, anniversaries), or just ordinary (holidays, annual events)—but are all the more meaningful because you've acknowledged them.

You know you have arrived when something major happens in your client's life and you are one of the first people to receive the news. You are now a trusted advisor and part of their inner circle. What an honor, and how special is the responsibility that comes from being this close confidant.

Seven-Step Discovery Process

The skills discussed earlier—communication, being an intuitive listener, emotional intelligence, asking compelling and thought-provoking questions—all come together for the discovery meeting. The meeting itself is a seven-step process, but the first and most important step is establishing your potential client's trust and respect.

1. The location of the meeting should be comfortable and in a nice-looking space with lots of natural light. You may want to rethink artificial flowers or plants. Your first few sentences should acknowledge why this meeting is taking place—to explore working together. Seat the prospect at the head of the table. Always have water or coffee in the room, with some cookies, fruit, or pastries. Someone should meet your clients in the lobby when they arrive. After all, this is not a doctor's office—the waiting time should be zero.

2. Explain how long the meeting will be, and walk through an agenda. Stop regularly and see if they have any questions.

3. Introductions are very important—introduce the team with enthusiasm and briefly include everyone's title, role, experience, and so forth, in plain English, no acronyms or "Wall Street" jargon.

4. Have a guide in front of you (the diagram in this chapter) but don't use it to read off one question at a time like you're checking off a list. The Q&A should have a conversational feel. The prospect will pick up on

what is not being said, body language, eye contact, and so on, as much as you will. However, someone on the team should take copious notes.

5. Your goal is to build trust and to quickly assess if you and your team can add value. Is this a good fit for your business model? Can you meet or exceed expectations? Don't try to be all things to all people. In the long run you both lose.

6. Get a commitment for a next meeting. Explain what you will focus on in the next meeting. Remind them of your consultative process and that you're in the business of building long-term, mutually beneficial relationships.

7. Always give the prospects the last word. Make sure they have had all their questions answered. Make those emotional deposits. Give them some marketing material and walk them to the elevator, or better yet their car. The small things I keep talking about.

Since this meeting is the most important meeting between client and advisor, I'm going to highlight the most common mistakes that I have seen over the years. Regardless of the channel, here are some of the mistakes:

- You're not well prepared for the meeting. You can Google anyone.
- You don't understand their world. If they are a business owner, do you understand their challenges?
- You talk too much, but don't ask the right questions. Dig deeper by peeling back the layers.
- You don't introduce (or provide poor introductions of) the rest of the team members and your handoffs to them are poor.

- You use too much industry language.
- You are unaware of how body language, facial expressions, and tone and rhythm (yours and theirs) affect the energy in the room.
- You allow the client to lead the meeting, and as a result the meeting is not as productive as it should be.
- You forget the saying, "Don't judge a book by its cover." Don't be so quick to draw conclusions regarding who you think the client is.
- You make too many assumptions regarding what the client is saying and what you're hearing. You forget to peel the onion. For example asking follow-up questions, what do you mean by that? Please tell me more.
- Missed opportunities to genuinely recognize the prospect for their accomplishments or what they are most proud of.

Chapter 17

A Question of Value, Not Price

"Knowing yourself is the beginning of all wisdom."
—*Aristotle*

Fee compression is felt by wealth managers and asset managers alike. Technology has created substantial disruption and it will continue. Amazon, Uber, Airbnb, Facebook, Netflix, Alibaba, Snapchat, Apple, Google, Waze, and so on. They all challenged the status quo. Commoditization by definition means you could only compete on price. Therefore trying to compete on price in the advice business is like Ritz Carlton trying to compete on price. Instead, focus on increasing value and prioritizing that value to different clients. A team with a $200 million book may have the opportunity to gain four to five times more assets through referral opportunities or by gathering additional client assets from competitor firms. Once you view the math from a big-picture perspective, it may help you see the overall value of a single client. The future will force the advisor to look and feel more like a family office. Protecting your price starting by understanding the value of each client relationship. The research goes on to say that the following elements in the *Harvard Business Review*, September 2016, the cover "What Does Your Customer Really Want?" Product and services deliver fundamental elements of value that address four kinds of needs: functional, emotional, life-changing, and social impact.

One way of evaluating and fine-tuning your client base further is by studying it from a sociological perspective. American demographics are changing so rapidly that the future wealth advisor will need to fully understand the distinctions among many highly segmented groups of investors. Targeting specific subgroups within your client base, such as those who are ready to transfer wealth, sell their business, or expand their business, will prove vital to your future success. The wealthy want value, and advisors who don't understand that will lose market share. A wealthy client will not think twice to spend $500 on a bottle of wine, but will negotiate hard when purchasing a new car. In the absence of value, price will always be an issue. You are the product or solution, not the stocks and bonds or money managers you recommend or the financial plan you create. You will not win business when you underestimate your value. However, if you demonstrate competence, project confidence, and act with integrity, your clients will feel comfortable discussing their financial needs with you and will pay for outstanding service and customized solutions. They will not pay for cookie-cutter solutions and incompetent people delivering inconsistent service.

The "Fee" Discussion

These are some of the explanations of the fees you charge. Many of the services are not visible to the client but it's your responsibility to be transparent about what they are and how they serve the client's interests. The services include:

- Creating a customized and comprehensive financial plan
- Asset allocation
- Manager review
- Risk management
- Tax efficiency considerations
- Performance reporting
- Rebalancing
- Overall account monitoring
- Customized estate planning services
- Insurance reviews
- Tailored college planning
- Banking and specialty financing
- Managing the client's philanthropic/giving strategy
- A team of experts dedicated to helping clients achieve their financial goals—personalized and proactive to meet client's objectives

Client Segmentation

Client segmentation is about identifying what type of client you want to service and how to deliver value to each segment. In order to fully appreciate why segmentation is important and works well we need to go back to 1897. We

Elements of Advisor Value

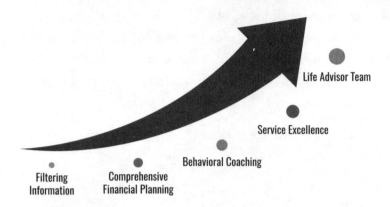

all have heard of the 80/20 rule. The person who defined this pattern was Vilfredo Pareto, an Italian economist examining patterns of wealth and income in nineteenth-century England. His research showed that roughly 80 percent of England's wealth was in the hands of 20 percent of the people. His real discovery came in the consistent mathematical relationship between the percentage of the population and the percentage of wealth they possessed. He found that this correlation existed not only in England, but throughout Europe.

In 1949, Harvard professor George Zipf called the 80/20 rule the principle of least effort. He stated that 20 to 30 percent of productive resources like people–time skills will consistently account for 70 to 80 percent of the activity related to that resource. This principle is seen every day in wealth management. Typically, 20 percent of your clients generate 80 percent of your revenue. In some cases, it may be 30 percent/70 percent, but the general theory holds as true today as it did in the nineteenth century. Therefore, client segmentation is about creating efficiency, capacity, discipline, and consistent process and growing your practice. Most importantly, it's about giving clients exceptional service and an outstanding experience.

I see the best teams fully embrace this concept. Yet, the majority of advisors do not segment their client-service model often because they do not understand the advantages to segmentation from both the client and business standpoints. Ultimately, client segmentation is about offering the highest standards of client experience and helping every client get the exceptional service they expect. It's finding the right balance of those clients being served in order for you to exceed expectations. Segmentation is as much art as it is science. The categories you use to segment your client base should include both objective and subjective categories. Revenue per client is an important component of segmentation but not the only one. For example, you may decide to segment based on:

- Client revenue
- Client assets
- Advocate—COI
- Likability
- Profitability
- Opportunity for future growth

Client segmentation can be achieved through various approaches but any wealth manager branding efforts should start early. Establishing account minimums sets ground rules and helps convey to a new client that you are a serious advisor and you both have certain expectations for the relationship.

The Elite Advisor Growth Model
- Individual model:
  - Execution
  - Competency
  - Mindset
  - Purpose
- Business model:
  - Business development
  - Client experience
  - Wealth management
  - Practice management

Advocates, Clients, and Prospects

Another way to segment clients is to think of them in three categories: advocates, clients, and prospects. As the Pareto Rule reminds us, 80 percent of our business derives from 20 percent of our clients. Those who are grouped in the top 20 percent are your advocates and they will receive 80 percent of your attention. They are walking billboards for your practice and can create a steady stream of referrals for you. They hardly ever question your recommendations. Clients are those who give you a healthy portion of their business, and they accept and value your advice. Prospects maintain a small portion of assets with you and lack a meaningful relationship with your practice. Segmenting your current client base this way can help you focus your attention effectively and even tell you when to let certain clients go if they prove to be too time-consuming or don't value your advice. Trying to please clients that simply don't value what you and your team deliver can be exhausting. Part ways, because you are detracting from your other clients.

If you manage your clients as you would manage a high-profile portfolio of investments, then you would rightfully expect that your energies would pay off in the long run. However, as suggested by Gupta and Lehmann in *Managing Your Customers as Investments: The Strategic Value of Customers in the Long Run*, there are two sides to customer value: the value a firm provides to a customer and the value of a customer to a firm. The first part represents your investment of time, energy, and resources and the second part is the actual return on this investment. Gupta and Lehmann segment clients into four categories: stars, lost causes, vulnerables, and free riders.

- Star clients are those who derive high value from the products and services you offer. You gain from them profitability, loyalty, and a longer retention time.
- Lost-cause clients are those who do not perceive great value in what you offer. Here you only gain when they transact on a large sale. If you are unable to migrate these customers to higher levels of profitability, reassigning or letting go of these accounts may be the best option.
- Vulnerable clients provide high value to the firm but do not receive value in return. They are vulnerable and prone to defect to competitors unless corrective action is taken quickly. These clients can be saved through better product offerings, additional services, and concerted support.

- Free riders are those who receive superior value from the products and services you offer, but provide little value to you. These customers exploit their relationship with you and your support staff, but return little ROI.

It Takes Two

Not every client–advisor relationship works or is worth investing in. Successful advisors know this and are able to navigate these difficult situations because they know themselves and they know and respect their own value as much as they do that of their clients. Acknowledging in these circumstances that you are not the solution is a solution in and of itself. If the advisor feels he or she cannot work well with a client, then the advisor should consult with his or her branch manager to see what action can be taken. Another advisor or another firm may be a better fit. If a client has unrealistic expectations or repeatedly asks you to discount your fees, he or she clearly does not value you and the services you provide. If you repeatedly oblige this client, then you are undervaluing your own business. But if you select your clients based on your business model and your philosophy, you are likely to achieve an incredibly high level of client loyalty and a subsequently steady stream of referrals. You are their solution, but also remember you can't be all things to all people.

It's a Multigenerational Business

The wealth management business is both art and science and the best practitioners draw on both to build and deepen client relationships. Very often, the client relationship is with the head of the household and does not extend to the spouse and children. Without having a strong relationship with all members of the family, you could be in jeopardy of losing the account if the decision-maker passes on. You will likely scramble to keep these accounts despite years of solid relationship-building with the now-deceased client. This generation is the richest ever, forecasted by one wealth management company to peak at about $54 trillion in assets by 2030. These baby boomers will live longer, healthier, and live more active lives than their parents or any previous generation. Boomers began retiring earlier this decade and roughly 10,000 boomers are retiring daily. This transfer of wealth should be part of the overall business plan. Relationships take a long time to build; therefore, start building touchpoints with the clients' children on a regular basis.

Meeting family members early in the process is vital. Employing a multigenerational focus will help you maintain and grow your asset base. Advisors can address these issues proactively by developing a well-rounded team that will cater to different aspects of the client's life, as well as to the family members. If you focus your team's time appropriately on the right clients, then you will recover the value of your investment and enjoy greater profitability in the long run.

I first met Sid Queler in 2015 when I held several programs throughout the country for his firm on growing the business. Sid is the head of business development at Atlantic Trust and has been in the industry for over 25 years. He leads a motivated team of professionals across 14 offices nationwide. Like myself, Sid is a family man and enjoys spending his time away from the office with his family.

Here is a question-and-answer about growing assets under management (AUM).

Rick: What's the firm's strategy and steps to grow AUM?

Sid: Our strategy is to keep what we have and build upon that. Client retention is our first priority and growth is a very close second. We realize that to grow we must build off of a stable base, which includes a very high client retention rate. That being said, we are laser-focused on growth. Our strategy is very personalized to not only the business development officers but the relationship managers as well. Each office will have a different strategy utilizing the building blocks that the firm provides. Each year we define our building blocks for growth. The six to ten building blocks will vary from year to year, taking into account the wealth management landscape. We implement a specific plan for the office utilizing the building blocks and then break it down even further. Business development officers have their own plan and relationship managers have their plan. We have found that including relationship managers/advisors in the growth plan has helped our growth significantly. As with any plan, accountability and monitoring is important but we want our professionals to have an entrepreneurial spirit and ownership so that they can execute on their plan.

Rick: What do you believe distinguishes a high performer?

Sid: Integrity, vision, and effort. If a professional at any level can operate at all times with the highest level of integrity, you may not always win the business but certainly know that you worked through the process in the "right way."

It is very hard to teach integrity but it is an invaluable trait. Next, you have to have a vision. Know where you are going and how you are going to get there. No one ever had a vision of going on a Sunday drive and getting somewhere. It takes effort. It is also hard to teach effort. After a while, we all start to sound the same in our business. So, who is going to outwork the competitor? I tell my team all the time that making another phone call, holding that last meeting late at night, driving those extra miles, or hopping on a plane to meet a client's child will pay off in many ways although most likely not immediately. Work with integrity, work with a vision and a purpose, and outwork everyone else and you will succeed in this business.

Rick: In addition to compensation and bonuses, what other methods do you use to recognize and reward high achievers?

Sid: I have found that high achievers value a personal touch. Yes, it's nice to have a high level of compensation but there is more to success than that. I like to meet face to face with my high achievers and discuss their success. I have found that having one-on-one dinners with high achievers goes a long way. They enjoy the fact that I have taken the time to spend alone with them on a personal level, which may or may not include their spouse. Those who don't shy away from the spotlight will be featured on firm-wide conference calls or publications both inside and outside the firm.

Rick: What's your process for engaging a high-net-worth client? What do you lead with and why?

Sid: That's a great question and there is no easy answer. Most potential clients are all looking for something different so you don't want to get involved in a closed-end discussion. Depending on the situation, my approach may differ, but I have learned that the most reliable way to engage is to speak about their family. It is usually a good starting point as the conversation tells you a lot about what is important to the individual. It also allows you to direct the conversation in many different ways. You learn a lot from prospective clients when they talk about their family and the conversation can go anywhere. Instead of asking about one individual, you are asking about a unit, which should result in a mutual connection. The only downside is that if the prospective client does not have a family, you need to be able to transition to another question right away. The best way to show value is during the discovery meeting. Remember not everyone will subscribe to your value proposition. Select your clients because if someone does not value your services it will be a tumultuous relationship.

Chapter 18

You Are the Solution

"Too many people overvalue what they are not and undervalue what they are."

—*Malcolm Forbes*

As Mark Twain said "The two most important days in your life are the day you are born and the day you find out why." Why am I dedicating a whole chapter on emphasizing that the advisor is the solution? Because we spend a disproportionate amount of time on products, platform, price, tools, technology, marketing, and so on. These things are not differentiators, they are important and foundational, but people buy people. They do business with people they like and trust.

I know that for many people, finding their calling in life can be a frustrating journey. For those who do find that perfect job or passion, you can see it in their eyes. You can see that they love what they do. When clients can see that passion, they see why you do what you do. Since you are ultimately what the client is buying, it may help to discover how you can be more passionate for your business and how you can create a brand that's more aligned with who you truly are. For some, the statement, "You are the solution," makes perfect sense, but others may immediately begin shaking their head. But what does "You are the solution" really mean? Start by thinking about your brand. When it comes to well-known brands like BMW, Nike, and Apple, we all feel and think something when these companies come up in an ad or in conversation. We all have certain expectations of their products. When I think of Ritz Carlton, I think classy, professional, and ladies and gentlemen serving ladies and gentlemen. I expect my expectations will be met or exceeded when I am staying at one of their properties. If I shop at Norstrom's I have an expectation.

When your clients think of you and your brand, what comes to mind? After meeting with a prospect for the first time, what three words will she use to describe you after the meeting? Are you sure that the way you see yourself is aligned with the way clients or team members see you? Whatever brand you think you are, take a step back and make sure to ask for feedback. The goal is for you or your firm to be viewed exactly as you want to be viewed. You are the solution; people buy you.

What's Your Likability Index?

Since people began transacting business, people have preferred to do business with people they like and share similar values. Far too many advisors put on masks when they meet with clients because they are leery of revealing their true person. They are afraid of being vulnerable. But being vulnerable, showing that you are not superhuman, that you have fears, that you have made mistakes, is an essential part of showing your client your humility. Why is that so important? By definition the phrase *value add* means something that's above ordinary. And because you are the solution, you have the ability to be different since the product itself can't be different. Plus, once the *real you* shows up, the client is more likely to open up and reveal her true goals and aspirations. So the only way for you to be the solution is to start by being authentic. When tempered with competence and confidence, successful advisors are as comfortable showing vulnerability as they are in highlighting their successes.

Personalized Service Matters

Personalized service and customized solutions are the chief ways to keep affluent clients happy. While it may be more convenient to do business over the phone or via email, you build a higher level of trust when you truly understand a client's fears, dreams, and their hoped-for legacies. This kind of relationship can only develop when you are sitting directly across from someone on a regular basis, not just once a year.

If you are working for one of the top-10 firms in the world with a strong brand image, you may have an initial competitive edge. Through millions of marketing and advertising dollars, their branding strategy creates the perception of trust, professionalism, integrity, and leadership, which may have helped in bringing the client to the firm in the first place. Although this may initially give you a foot in the door, it is the way you conduct yourself and run your business that will very quickly become the image your clients associate with your firm. They trust in you to make sense of the volumes of information and plethora of products they are offered and to consistently scan the universe to seek out the best solutions for them. In the eyes of your clients, you are ultimately the brand or product—the solution—in which they are investing. This leads you to clearly articulate who you are, what you do, and what makes you different. I strongly encourage you to do this exercise with your team. You need to think about the questions as they pertain to your model specifically, but I provide you with sample questions and answers so you can see the exercise in action. (Don't take a shortcut and just copy what I wrote here. You will only reap the benefits by building the answers in a collaborative environment with your team.) Believe in what you come up with, articulate it with passion and speed, and, most important, be able to deliver on it.

Who are we?

We are a team of experts dedicated and passionate to serve high-net-worth clients and institutions. We work collaboratively to bring the best solutions to our client.

What do we do?

We help individuals achieve their financial goals by delivering customized wealth strategies solutions. We provide peace of mind by proactively understanding your needs and working tirelessly to exceed your expectations. We do not push product.

How do we do it?

Our client-centric and solutions-driven philosophy starts with a deep understanding of our clients' goals, objectives, dreams, and aspirations. We deliver a customized plan and service model based on this discovery meeting and ongoing dialogue. Our customized and comprehensive wealth plan guides our strategy and tactical plan. We monitor progress to the client's specific plan and adjust it to keep pace with any changes in the client's life.

Whom do we serve?

Our model, expertise, and team focus on high-networth individuals and institutions that demand more customized and personalized attention. We work with entrepreneurs, accounting firms, senior executives, and specifically women executives.

What makes us different?

We deliver a truly integrated wealth management offering and world-class service excellence. We pay attention to the smallest details and we are passionate to help you reach your goals. Our team approach gives you the depth and breadth of a complete life plan and we are with you side by side on the journey.

The Six Cs of Loyalty

A study of 1,417 affluent clients conducted by industry researchers Russ Alan Prince and David A. Geracioti revealed that wealth managers can create client loyalty by focusing on the six *C*s:

1. *Character:* Integrity is the most important quality for all clients; they must believe that their advisor is honest at all times.
2. *Chemistry:* Advisors must be in sync with their clients. The advisor and client should share similar values and can quickly and easily connect on an emotional level.
3. *Caring:* The reassurance that the advisor really knows the client's goals and objectives.
4. *Competence:* The perception that the advisor is a smart and respected professional in the field.
5. *Cost-Effectiveness:* The belief that the client is receiving genuine value for the cost of the service and products provided.
6. *Consultative Insights:* The definition of the entire advisor–client relationship as an ongoing partnership over time and, as such, probably the most important factor. Wealthy clients prefer a collaborative relationship. An advisor can build loyalty by contacting these clients appropriately (not just concerning their money) and customizing any communication, as such clients are not interested in generic off-the-shelf presentations.

These six *C*s can help shape, define, and communicate the advantages of the most important product you are selling—yourself. Building loyalty is also about managing client expectations. Ultimately, the wealth management process should include a commitment to contact clients a minimum of 18 times a year. According to Prince and Geracioti, this level of contact results in the greatest level of client satisfaction and loyalty, as well as the greatest likelihood of receiving additional assets and ongoing referrals.

Chapter 19

Getting Into Flow

"Your vision will become clear only when you look into your heart. Who looks outside, dreams. Who looks inside, awakens."

—*Carl Jung*

In order to achieve optimal performance, regularly ask yourself, "Am I running the business, or is the business running me? Am I still having fun? Am I being challenged? Have I just become complacent?" Advisors are often asked to put together a business plan outlining their vision, overall plan, strategy, and tactics for attracting clients and assets. It would be wiser if advisors were asked to put together a life plan, one that would include the impact of their business on their personal, social, and spiritual life.

Ask yourself:

- What do I value most in life?
- What drives me?
- What principles guide my decisions?

- What do I ultimately want to achieve in my life?
- What's my mission in life?
- What's my vision of my future?
- What inspires me?
- Am I living my life or am I still living the life one of my parents wanted? (Set yourself free and seek a new challenge.)

Creating a life plan helps you keep all aspects of who you are in perspective and allows you to measure your performance based on truly important goals. Naturally, you should adjust your life accordingly when those objectives aren't met, but it's also essential to reward yourself and your family when you do attain your goals.

What Is Success to You?

"Don't aim at success. The more you aim at it and make it a target, the more you are going to miss it. For success, like happiness, cannot be pursued; it must ensue, and it only does so as the unintended side effect of one's personal dedication to a cause greater than oneself or as the by-product of one's surrender to a person other than oneself. Happiness must happen, and the same holds for success: you have to let it happen by not caring about it."

—*Victor E. Frankl*

Success means different things to different people. You may measure success by wealth, performance, fulfillment, or some combination of all three. Wealth is not just money. It is a mindset. It is a set of thoughts. When you maintain a balance at home, in personal relationships, in your health, and at work, you have created an optimal foundation for wealth-driven performance. You now have the right energy.

If you approach difficulties with a balanced perspective, you will be able to weather them more easily and succeed over the long haul. Advisors who have been in the business for a number of years understand the industry can be an emotional rollercoaster with many ups and a fair number of downs. Over the years, the business makes you wiser and humbler—if you learn from your mistakes. Some advisors seek the support of other advisors, managers, or mentors to discuss their challenges and life goals and keep their overall perspective in balance.

It all begins with purpose. Once you define your purpose, the purpose will serve as your ongoing energy and motivation. Once that is clearly defined, you move to your mindset, which is your belief system, to competency, which is your expertise, and then to execution, which is how you persevere.

Discovering Your Purpose

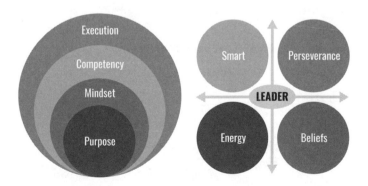

Stay Grounded

Remember what is, is, and what is not, is not. For many successful advisors, this is the mantra that changes—or grounds—their lives. In other words, they understand what they can control and what they cannot. They also understand the difference between cause and effect and the difference between making things happen versus allowing things to happen to you. Stephen Covey said it best: "I am not the product of my circumstances. I'm a product of my decisions." Getting emotional about situations or circumstances you cannot do anything about is a waste of good energy and time. With so much information at our disposal, both as advisors and clients we need perspective and

Brain Hacking

Strategically allocating
your time to focus on:

PERSPECTIVE vs INFORMATION

EFFECTIVE vs BUSY

know-how to effectively manage our time and avoid falling into the black hole of data overload.

> "The only person over whom you have direct and immediate control is yourself. The most important assets to develop, preserve and enhance, therefore, are your own capabilities. And no one can do it for you— you must cultivate the habits of leadership effectiveness for yourself—and doing so will be the single best investment you'll ever make."
>
> —*Stephen R. Covey*

Keep Your Head in the Game

The most successful advisors derive great satisfaction from what they do. In part, this is because they often perform their work in a state of optimal performance, what psychologist Mihaly Csikszentmihalyi calls "flow."

Csikszentmihalyi defines flow as being fully absorbed in an activity to the point where one's sense of time is lost and feelings of great satisfaction are experienced. If you are performing in flow, you have a sense of energized focus in which one thought follows another quickly and effortlessly and you experience full involvement and a feeling that you are using your skills to the utmost. Clearly, it is an immensely fulfilling place to be. If you strive to achieve your own flow, you will discover what truly makes you happy and what specific activities help you maintain your flow.

Notably, flow occurs when both the challenges experienced and the level of skill necessary to meet or overcome them are high.

CHARACTERISTICS OF FLOW

- Clear goals (expectations and rules are discernible and goals are attainable and align appropriately with one's skill set and abilities).
- Concentration and focus, a high degree of concentration on a limited field (a person engaged in the activity will have the opportunity to focus and to delve deeply into it).
- A loss of the feeling of self-consciousness.
- Distorted sense of time. One's subjective experience of time is altered.
- Direct and immediate feedback (successes and failures in the course of the activity are apparent, so that behavior can be adjusted as needed).
- Balance between ability level and challenge (the activity is neither too easy nor too difficult).
- A sense of personal control over the situation or activity.
- The activity is intrinsically rewarding, so there is an effortlessness of action.
- People become absorbed in their activity and focus of awareness is narrowed down to the activity itself: action–awareness merging.

Source: Csikszentmihalyi (1975), p. 72

Symbiosis

Clearly, achieving real success requires a symbiotic relationship between your work and personal life. Overlooking

Optimal Performance Occurs When Both Variables Are High

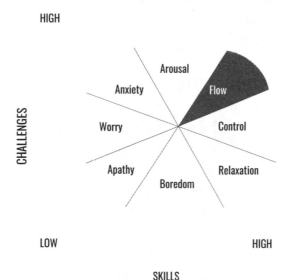

Source: Massimini & Carli; Csikszentmihalyi (1990)

the effect your personal life has on your business is short-sighted. Equally important, you should share your life plan with those around you who have a direct effect on your well-being so they understand what you are trying to achieve. Family support is vital. Your loved ones have a vested interest in your success. By respecting the balance between your work life and your personal life, you can achieve a greater measure of physical, emotional, and spiritual harmony and enjoy even greater satisfaction and success.

Advice for the New Advisor

- Start with your vision: Who are you? What do you hope to accomplish?

- Be honest with yourself and others. Live your life, not someone else's.
- Be conscious of your beliefs and biases—they may be holding you back.
- Discover your talent as an advisor and become the best you can be.
- The law of proximity: find people who can help you and learn from them. You cannot get to the right place being around the wrong people.
- Persistence, heart, and the right attitude will give you a competitive advantage.
- Play with confidence and always look to improve and build competencies.
- Be enthusiastic and positive, especially after a letdown. Have the courage to get back up.
- Build a large network and be seen as a giver. It will serve you well.
- Understand that happiness is not based on possessions, power, prestige, or fame.
- Take full responsibility for your success and your decisions. You create, promote, and allow what goes on in your environment. Don't be a victim of circumstance. Don't ever tolerate a bad environment and bullies.
- Be forgiving of yourself and others. You will make mistakes. Learn and move on. Don't allow yourself to be defined by the past.
- Become an effective communicator with a high level of emotional intelligence.
- Be grateful, compassionate, and generous. You will never win the *more* game.

- Have a sense of curiosity and be inspired to learn every day.
- Find the right mentors. The best mentors ask lots of questions and listen well.
- Always put your clients' interest before everyone else's. But never compromise your integrity.

Chapter 20

Change Is Difficult

"If the rate of change on the outside exceeds the rate of change on the inside, then the end is near."

—*Jack Welch*

We know today the rate of change in the wealth management industry is eclipsing most organizations and they are struggling to keep up. In *Good to Great: Why Some Companies Make the Leap . . . and Others Don't*, author Jim Collins said, "Good is the enemy of great." It takes a tremendous amount of courage and maturity to change the status quo, especially when the status quo is pretty good. However, if you're not moving forward in this business, you will soon find yourself overtaken at best and hurtling backward at worst. There is no room in the wealth management industry for being static or passive. The universe of financial products and services continues to expand, which makes keeping up with technology and product innovation an absolute necessity.

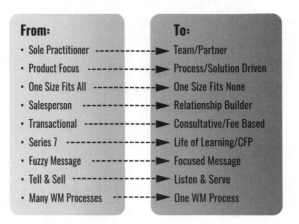

From:		To:
• Sole Practitioner	---------->	Team/Partner
• Product Focus	---------->	Process/Solution Driven
• One Size Fits All	---------->	One Size Fits None
• Salesperson	---------->	Relationship Builder
• Transactional	---------->	Consultative/Fee Based
• Series 7	---------->	Life of Learning/CFP
• Fuzzy Message	---------->	Focused Message
• Tell & Sell	---------->	Listen & Serve
• Many WM Processes	---------->	One WM Process

Defy Complacency

Advisors who have experienced relatively good production and performance and are satisfied with their current
income tend to stop prospecting and, as a result, their
business plateaus after about eight years. The asset growth
of most advisors is flat-to-negative year after year because
they get comfortable and start to coast. Defying complacency requires you to constantly redefine your business,
goals, and who your most profitable clients are. You may
have to create a new business model, change your infrastructure, or seek advanced training in areas in which you
or your team may be lacking in order to move forward
with a continuous sense of momentum. John F. Kennedy
said it well: "Effort and courage are not enough without
purpose and direction." The war of whether or not your
business plateaus is won or lost between your ears. Discover

purpose again to provide the energy necessary to get you moving in the right direction.

Those with thriving businesses never become complacent; they reinvent themselves every three or four years and are constantly evolving through personal and professional growth. Above all, they never stop learning. They look for every opportunity to gain an edge: reading, attending seminars and workshops, hiring personal coaches, and networking with other smart professionals. This lifetime commitment of learning is not a part-time activity, nor is it for the faint-hearted. It takes total dedication. But it is both valuable and worthwhile on every level and, ultimately, the difference between thriving as a wealth management professional or plateauing and declining.

Set Goals

Goal setting is the very core of what drives our ambition, whether it is in business, life, or sports. Goals should be specific, measurable, and achievable. The outcome must be clear, quantifiable, and in harmony with our purpose. Over the years I have learned to modify my original goals because circumstances change. Staying focused on the big goals is what matters most.

Goal setting consists of five steps:

1. Objectively look at your total picture and determine where you want to go to improve your life.
2. Decide why you want to achieve this particular goal. What will it mean to you?

3. How and when are you going to do this? What's the timeline and what are the milestones?

4. Who is going to help you stay on track and be supportive?

5. Take action, get started, and reward yourself when you achieve your goal.

Setting goals helps us measure our progress and stay on course to achieve our desired aim. If we are not moving closer to our target, then we must reevaluate and change our course of action to get back on track.

It is essential to set medium-term goals in order to bridge the gap between our short- and long-term goals. Medium-term goal setting provides you with additional encouragement and motivates you to continue the journey. Design a reward system. A reward doesn't have to be big, just something to celebrate your achievements. If you don't reach your intended goals as planned, don't punish yourself. Playing the win/lose game causes us to lose sight of what we are really trying to accomplish. If we adopt a flexible approach to achieving the desired outcome, instead of following a rigid path, then we are capable of addressing the bumps in the road without feeling daunted. It is okay to revisit and rethink how you are going to achieve results. Setting clear goals and having the confidence and courage to take action will help you overcome obstacles.

Conquer Fear

We know by studying successful people that high performers fail all the time. They take calculated risks, learn from their mistakes, and then move forward. This healthy blend of confidence and humility is fueled by a strong vision of where they would like to be and failing is viewed as just a detour on the path to success. When you just focus on the outcome you live in a state of constant anxiety. Once you do the best you can, you need nature to take its course. For example, you just finished your fourth meeting with a prospect and now you're waiting for him to make a decision about whether he will move his account or not. At this point the decision is out of your control and any energy you spend on thinking about it is a waste of good energy. Your head may still be thinking of a different tactic or approach but, as you know, pushing is not effective and often will backfire.

As Tania Kotsos wrote in her book, *The Secret to Effortless Detachment,*

> Detachment from the outcome you want to experience is vital to creating your ideal reality. To be attached is to live in the fear that what you want will not materialize and traps you in a continuous state of desire. Attachment to anything or anyone turns love into fear and belief into doubt.

Unsuccessful People Never Fail Because They Never Try

Too many people don't try because they are afraid that they will fall and not have the courage and confidence to get back up. In contrast, high achievers pay no attention to this scoreboard mentality. They do not tally how many times one succeeds versus fails. They are not driven by the desire to be accepted. They are driven by a greater purpose, which is to reach their full potential and "play to win," while others "play not to lose." It's a big difference and the resulting impact on their practices is tremendous. Because they are open to possibilities, they try new things and keep on growing.

Successful individuals are attracted to the wealth management industry because they can run their business in a flexible, entrepreneurial way and make a substantive difference in people's lives. This gives many of them tremendous satisfaction while building personal wealth for themselves and their clients.

As Colin Powell eloquently said, "There are no secrets to success: it is the result of preparation, hard work and learning from failure." Once you determine you would like to grow your business by 20 or 30 percent over the next several years, you must ask yourself more in-depth questions and explore how others have achieved their success. This process will allow you to make the journey from good to great without the fear of taking a step back or misstepping. A few years ago I had the opportunity to hear Colin Powell speak in New York to a small group of leaders. I asked him about mistakes and motivating people. He quickly responded by first saying that "You cannot motivate people; they can only motivate themselves." As for mistakes he said, "In my line of work we make mistakes all the time, but you need to move on and not live in the past." Certainly insightful words to live by.

Succession Planning

Succession planning is a challenge for many advisors. And, frankly, it doesn't matter if you're at a wirehouse or the founder of a large RIA. If you truly want to move from good to great, you need to think about the most important piece of the puzzle: human capital. It's key to attracting the best talent not only to help you take your business to the next level, but also to make sure your business and legacy lives on. The 300,000 advisors in the business now are getting older; the average advisor is about 56 years old. Therefore, if you would like to have more free time after spending 25-plus years building your business, start to work just as hard identifying top talent to take over for you when you retire or semi-retire.

The biggest issue I see is this: most advisors expect the right talent, the right fit, the passionate successor to fall in their lap. They often misjudge how much effort it takes to identify that top talent, the right fit. The smart advisors running very successful RIAs look for a successor CEO and over time give him equity into the firm. You must have the courage to relinquish that control when the time has come. Don't be afraid to hire people smarter than you.

Change Is Difficult but Not Changing Is Fatal

"Don't measure yourself by what you have accomplished, but by what you should have accomplished with your ability."

—*John Wooden*

For the confident advisor, embracing change is an opportunity to grow. For others, however, change may be intimidating because they are comfortable and fear what they may lose. There has always been stress and anxiety in our business; I would argue those levels are higher now more than ever. We have always been stressed about helping clients achieve their objectives, market volatility, change in management, and succession planning. The list goes on and on. With the lightning-fast pace of just about everything today, we usually feel we are in survival mode. We make decisions based on habits and beliefs that may not be in our long-term best interest. In other words, choosing to change and be happy is not a natural state for most of us.

We must discover a better path. Choose to live with gratitude. Embrace personal growth. We are privileged to be in this business and must accept the awesome responsibility we have to serve our clients. We have the power to choose. Advisors with a growth mindset cultivate a state of mind from which they choose to create healthy change in their lives. They choose happiness over victimhood. Be committed to growth and be committed to live in joy and possibilities. This fulfillment can only happen if you take full responsibility for your circumstances.

Advisors may be resistant to a new business model, new technology, new products or services, or a new team formation. But savvy clients will be aware of these advancements and keeping up with these trends will help you keep up with your clients and, even more importantly, ahead of your clients. Being aware of new trends isn't enough. The old adage, "knowledge is power," is only partially true. Turning knowledge into action is the real power.

It is often at this last step—action—where most advisors stumble. As Darwin said, it's not the most intelligent or strongest species that survive but those that are able to adapt, to evolve. I still see many advisors working with outdated skill sets.

Ultimately, successful advisors are not necessarily the ones with the impressive-sounding degrees. They are people who think on their feet, who genuinely like people, who communicate effectively, and who are always looking to improve their skills. They are the ones who have mastered the fundamentals and are relentless on executing. They are willing to change. For example, you would be surprised by the number of advisors who manage a large business of $500 million who still come into the office every other Saturday to review statements, catch up on reading reports, or plan the weeks ahead. It's a myth that we only made the extra effort when we first came into the business. The simple fact is this: elite advisors enjoy what they do and as a result work much harder than most. It may look easy from the outside, but when you spend some time with them you can quickly see they are logging more hours. They want to keep the momentum going and have no interest in moving backward.

Successful advisors know the value of a mentor. A true mentor offers an impartial view, builds confidence, is non-judgmental, and helps us push forward with our intended plans. You are never too old to be a mentor or to need a mentor. (Remember: successful advisors never stop learning.)

Many organizations spend millions of dollars on learning and development and run fairly effective programs, but that's not nearly enough to keep pace in this dynamic industry. It is up to the individual to stay at the forefront of changes that will affect their clients. Learning does not simply mean reading the *Wall Street Journal* or

Barron's. It is a lifelong process driven by a continual thirst for knowledge, a desire for improvement, and the ability to turn that knowledge into action. "Lifelong Learning" was the cover story of the January 14, 2017, issue of *The Economist.*

What Have You Done Lately?

Lifelong learning is continuous, never-ending learning. The degree you earned 10 years ago—never mind two or three decades back—is not enough. Consider what you've done recently to improve your practice or your performance. If you already have a highly effective team in place, what training have you done together to better serve the client? To create a better working environment, what technology or social media training have you had?

Many top advisors spend a considerable amount of money annually to improve their practice in one form or another. One of the best ways to learn is to teach, write a book or an article, or speak at community events. Curiosity drives learning and development and both keep you energized and relevant—and open to change. It forces you to be conscious of what's most important to you, your family, and your clients and also helps you to make informed decisions.

Part of what makes this business so interesting is the constant seismic shifts that signal new waves of change and innovation. In order to fully enjoy the journey and stay ahead of these changes, you must embrace a lifelong learning process.

Attitude Is Everything

No matter what business you are in, everyone has ups and downs that sometimes seem insurmountable. Viktor Frankl, Holocaust survivor and author of the classic memoir, *Man's Search for Meaning*, says we should banish the tendency to feel sorry for ourselves. We need a healthy focus. Why is it that some deal with crisis or setbacks better than others? Some bounce back even stronger. I am sure you have heard the old saying, "That which does not kill me makes me stronger." Whether you talk about sports or the corporate world, attitude and mental toughness surface often because of the staying power and obstacles one must go through to achieve his or her goals, to hold up under pressure, to go the extra mile despite being mentally exhausted. Once again the question is: Why are some able to press on and others are incapable and feel they are the victim?

The first time I heard the expression "mental toughness" was from my high school coach. At the time, all that meant to me was getting through triple sessions under a typical hot, humid, scorching August day with very little water. In recent years, it has meant staying focused while building my consulting business and being there for my family. It's staying active and healthy and never losing my curiosity and passion to explore not only the world but also my own human potential.

As advisors, occasionally we stray from responsibilities that come with a demanding job because we lack mental toughness or the right attitude. It takes an abundance of mental toughness to address change. It takes lots of courage to stay focused when things around you fall apart. Viktor Frankl, in his book, said it best: "He who has a 'why' to live can bear with almost any 'how'" As a Holocaust survivor, Frankl knows all too well that life holds meaning under even the most miserable circumstances. His experiences convinced him that a person is capable of defining and surmounting the worst conditions imaginable. Whether a person behaves with courage and dignity or succumbs to degradation depends on decisions, not conditions. That is mental toughness.

God willing, we will never know the likes of what Viktor Frankl experienced; however, we will go through difficulties in business and in life. Ultimately, you are one hundred percent responsible for your attitude. Don't blame anyone and don't be held hostage to a particular problem you might be going through. Make the best of life on a daily basis and remember that your attitude will ultimately be determined by the decisions you make—the changes you embrace—rather than outside circumstances. Once you admit that you are in charge of your life, you can take ownership and soar.

Chapter 21

Investment Management

As the term *wealth management* has become mainstream, more firms are moving toward a model that asks clients about life goals, liabilities, work, family, and spending patterns as a way to increase value. Managing money is just one part of the much bigger picture—although certainly it's a very significant part. The term *wealth management* was first used in 1933 and has become popular in the last 25 years. As more and more firms have started to focus on broader relationships, planning has become core just as portfolio construction. By standard definition, wealth management means serving the high-net-worth market, but everyone has their own definition of what wealth management means. The four stages to wealth management are wealth accumulation, wealth planning, wealth preservation, and wealth transfer. The big pillars of these stages are the risk tolerance of the client, time horizon, the risk/reward aspect

of each asset class, tax efficiency, and how each component fits with the overall plan. Wealth management and
investment management are not interchangeable.

Future clients will have more options on how they
invest. They will have a number of choices: do-it-yourself
robo, robo-assisted, advisor, and life advisor team.

Hindsight, as they say, is 20/20. I have witnessed and
felt the anxiety of many market corrections. My first was
the 1987 crash, followed by the technology bubble in 2000,
the liquidity crisis that began in 2007, and the deep recession that marked 2008/2009. All of these corrections have
provided me with a deeper understanding of not only who
I am as an investor, but the overall industry. As a student
of the business, I had a front-row seat to how advisors
and high-net-worth clients reacted to these volatile markets. So it begs the question, how can one avoid these setbacks? Some advisors respond to severe market corrections
by underweighting their equity portfolios. However, the
stock market's history for the past 200 years tells us betting
against America is a mistake.

From a historical perspective, the equity market returned
11.7 percent from 1928-2016. But we know the market is
never "average." Therefore, maintaining purchasing power
is key to maintaining your lifestyle. Stocks have lost at least
10 percent of their value 23 times in the last 122 years.
Understanding investors' risk tolerance is arguably the
most important thing you can discuss with your clients on
a regular basis. Waiting until a major correction occurs is an
expensive way of getting to know what a client can handle.
Some clients may only be comfortable with volatility

somewhere around 20 percent. History and wisdom is always the best way to think about the future and how to create wealth. When Warren Buffett was asked about his secret of creating a $67 billion fortune, he said, "My wealth has come from a combination of living in America, some lucky genes, and compound interest." As someone who's been invested in the market for the past 35 years I can tell you first hand that compound interest is indeed the secret—and avoiding big mistakes. The other major lesson we can learn from Warren Buffett is to stay in the market and ride its ups and downs. Furthermore, Buffett doesn't just buy stocks; he buys companies. Because even if you are smart enough to get out of the market at the right time, you also have to know when to get back in. Diversification is always your friend.

One of the best ways to add value for your clients is to reduce the noise around them. By noise, I am referring to the overload of information we receive on a daily basis. While some of the information is truly valuable and relevant to the client, much of it is written to stir the pot or create drama or even distract people from what's really going on. It's important that you know how to filter useful information from the noise. As their advisor, clients depend on you to help reduce their anxiety, not increase their blood pressure by providing noise that means nothing in the end. Historically, every four to six years we experience a 20-plus percent market correction. You must guide your clients through these times of volatility.

After 35 years I have learned that markets cannot be timed with any consistency. I have also learned that for the past 100 years equities have provided substantially better returns than other asset classes. What does the future hold? Well, no one knows. What we do know is this: history favors a return to the mean. Therefore, if an investor doesn't have at least a five-year time horizon, he probably has no business being in the equity market. As well, the world is getting more prosperous and emerging nations are experiencing growth of their middle class. We are living through a technological revolution that will fuel growth. Equities are needed to protect purchasing power. For many, being out of the market poses the biggest risk when it comes to portfolio construction. Far too many investors get scared out of the market at the worst time.

When I first started as an advisor in the early 1980s, I had a handful of clients who were wise investors and knew a great deal about building a portfolio. They understood why trying to time the market is a foolish thing to do and they knew the importance of dollar-cost averaging. These clients would invest in high-quality stocks on a regular basis, growing their overall portfolio. Over the years these clients became wealthy. I specifically remember one client, a New York police officer whose mother taught him how to invest in the market when he was in his twenties. As time went on he accumulated a net worth of over $4 million between some inheritance and smart investing. The market volatility didn't bother his generation of investors.

Today, advisors talk about goals-based wealth management, aligning an investment strategy by goals based on a particular time horizon. Successful portfolio construction must be based on the client's needs, wants, and legacy.

One way to think about structuring a portfolio is based on timeline segmentation. Long-term portfolios are those looking 10 to 15 years out, intermediate-term portfolios, 5 to 10 years, and near-term portfolios, 6 months to 2 years. If you have been in the business for a few years, you have seen data showing the benefits of remaining in the market. For example, from 1996 to 2015, the S&P 500 returned 8.18 percent, if fully invested. Missing the 10 best-performing market days during that period of time meant an investor's returns were cut by half to 4.49 percent. If an investor missed the 30 best days, his return declined to −0.05 percent. Trying to time the market is impossible. That's why a diversified portfolio can help you stay in the market and make the ride a little smoother.

From Stockbroker to Life Advisor

How did we move from the traditional account executive or stockbroker to financial advisor or wealth advisor? From the late 1970s and through the 1980s and 1990s, it was about firms manufacturing products and stockbrokers selling shares in those firms, be it stocks, bonds, closed-end funds, or limited partnerships. A guideline—Rule 405—required that brokers determine the suitability of investments before making recommendations. At the end of the day, it was about selling and earning a commission on the transactions, and doing what you thought was in your client's best interest. Today, the financial world is moving toward a fiduciary standard in which an advisor occupies a position of special trust and confidence when working with clients to act with undivided loyalty to the client. This includes disclosure of how the financial advisor is to be compensated and any other conflicts of interest. Regardless of how the rules surrounding the fiduciary standard change going forward, the future will demand that the advisor be completely transparent and always put the client's interests first.

As with everything there are risks that come with investing and managing another person's wealth. One can't talk about putting the clients' interests first if one does not have the skill, knowledge, and competency to understand risk. Clients want to maximize returns on a risk-adjusted basis. A little history on risk will serve us well, but for a deeper dive, I wholeheartedly recommend *Against the Gods* by Peter L. Bernstein, and, in my opinion, it should be mandatory reading for anyone in financial services.

The serious study of risk began during the Renaissance (1300–1700) when long-held beliefs were challenged and new ideas were introduced. It was a time of religious turmoil, nascent capitalism, and a vigorous approach to science and the future. In 1654, the Chevalier de Méré, a French nobleman with a taste for both gambling and mathematics, challenged the famed French mathematician Blaise Pascal to solve a puzzle. The question was how to divide the stakes of an unfinished game of chance between two players when one of them is ahead. The puzzle had confounded mathematicians since the time it was posed some one hundred years earlier by the monk and mathematician Luca Paccioli. Pascal turned for help to Pierre de Fermat, a lawyer who was also a brilliant mathematician. The outcome of their collaboration was intellectual dynamite, resulting in the theory of probability, the mathematical heart of the concept of risk.

The theory of probability enabled people for the first time to make decisions and forecast the future with the help of numbers. Fast forward to 1952, when Harry Markowitz, a young graduate student at the University of Chicago, demonstrated mathematically why putting all your eggs in one basket is an unacceptably risky strategy. Tony will discuss Harry Markowitz in my interview.

The word *risk* derives from the early Italian word, *risicare*, which means "to dare." In this sense, risk is a choice rather than a fate. The action we dare to take depends on how free we are to make choices. In his book, *Against the Gods*, Bernstein points out that persistent tension exists between those who assert that the best decision is based on quantification numbers, determined by the patterns of the past, and those who base their decisions on more subjective degrees of belief about the uncertain future. This push–pull dynamic has never been resolved and is inherent in understanding risk.

Helping a client understand risk beyond investments is helping the client make better choices and plan accordingly. The advisor of today and tomorrow is a life advisor, not a stockbroker selling a product. The biggest question you need to ask yourself is: What's the most efficient and cost-effective way to manage your client's portfolio? What is your talent? Are you a stock picker? Or are you a great asset allocator and play the role of the quarterback, hiring and firing money managers? Outsourcing investment management for most advisors is simply the way to run a business and most importantly the client's best solution.

To explore how the investing landscape is changing, I conducted an interview with a friend and former colleague, Tony Davidow. Tony has over 30 years of experience in the industry. He began his career working for a family office, later worked for a large wealth management firm as an asset manager, and is currently serving as an asset allocation strategist for the Schwab Center for Financial Research. He is an award-winning author and frequent speaker at industry conferences.

Rick: How has asset allocation and portfolio construction evolved over the last several decades, and how should advisors evolve their approach?

Tony: There are three macro-trends that advisors will need to address in order to continue to grow their practices and meet their clients' needs: (1) advisors will need to understand and embrace the role and use of nontraditional investments, (2) advisors will need to incorporate active and passive investing, and (3) advisors will need to incorporate some form of forward-looking tactical allocations.

Today's asset allocation needs to evolve beyond the old 60/40 portfolio (60 percent S&P 500 and 40 percent Barclays Aggregate Bond index). It used to be sufficient to use a basic stock, bond, and cash portfolio where your stocks provided growth, bonds provided income, and cash provided stability. However, the current market presents significant challenges for the 60/40 portfolio. Bond yields are at generationally low levels and stock returns will likely be below their historic norms.

In 1952, Harry Markowitz first introduced the concept of diversification, which later became the basis of Modern Portfolio Theory (MPT). Markowitz's work concluded that an investor could reduce the overall risk of a portfolio by including investments that have low correlations to one another. Markowitz once called this "the only free lunch in finance." In other words, diversification can deliver benefits over time at no additional cost.

Markowitz's research focused on diversification across a group of stocks. We now live in a global economy where companies sell goods and services around the world. The world is more complex, but fortunately we have more efficient ways of accessing the markets.

In order to reap the benefits of diversification, today's advisors need to expand the number of asset classes and include certain nontraditional investments. Stock allocations should include domestic large- and small-cap and international and emerging markets, among others. Bonds should be diversified across Treasuries, corporations, high yield, and international and emerging markets debt, among others. Investing in commodities, real estate, and alternative investments can provide broader diversification.

Rick: With the expanding number of asset classes, it may seem daunting to clients and advisors. How do you suggest advisors explain the merits of these investments?

Tony: You're right. Investors are often intimidated by the unknown so we suggest changing the manner in which advisors introduce some of these new investment options. You can think of a portfolio as a series of puzzle pieces. Viewing each piece in isolation may seem confusing— but when put together the right way, the picture comes into focus.

Investors understand goals and outcomes. If we change the discussion to outcomes, it's easier for investors to understand the role each investment plays in putting the pieces of the portfolio together. Growth will come primarily from stocks—U.S. large and small, international and emerging markets. Growth and income will come from dividend-paying stocks here and abroad, plus master limited partnerships (MLPS) and real estate investment trusts (REITs). Income will come primarily from fixed income—Treasuries, corporates, high yield, and so on. Certain investments have been effective in hedging the impact of inflation, like TIPS, REITs, and some commodities. Cash, gold, and Treasuries can serve as defensive assets. Not only is this approach easier for clients to understand but it helps in managing expectations.

Rick: For many years I've heard the debate "active" versus "passive," but you're suggesting that there is a role for both. Please explain your point of view. I know that you've done a lot of research on "smart beta" strategies. Are they active or passive?

Tony: For years, academics and advisors have debated the merits of "active" and "passive" strategies. Active management

A Portfolio Is Like a Puzzle

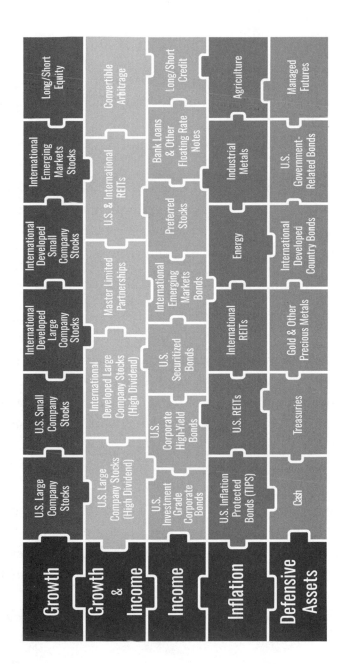

generally means a mutual fund or separately managed account (SMA). Passive management is generally in the form of an index-based mutual fund or exchange-traded fund (ETF).

The critics of active management would point to their difficulty in outperforming their passive benchmarks. Active managers would often counter with their skill in selecting winning companies, and avoiding the losers.

The popularity of indexing exploded after 2008 as advisors were challenged to justify the value of active management during the financial crisis. Most active managers were not able to outperform their benchmarks during the 2008 downturn. Today, there are over $3 trillion in ETF assets under management globally, providing exposure to virtually every segment of the market. Most of the major indexes, and most of the ETFs in the marketplace, are market-cap oriented, meaning they provide the largest weighting to the largest companies regardless of their financial strength. One might say a market-cap index "overweights the overvalued stocks and underweights the undervalued stocks."

The first generation of indexing was focused on replicating a particular benchmark in a cost-effective fashion, also known as "cheap beta." The second generation of indexing sought to improve upon the market experience, either increasing the return potential or reducing the risk. These strategies are often referred to as "smart beta" or "strategic beta." Smart beta strategies often leverage academic research showing that you could improve the market experience by breaking the link with price (i.e., the dependency on size). For example, fundamental index strategies screen and weight securities on such factors as sales, cash flow, and dividends + buybacks.

Smart beta strategies employ different weighting methodologies and periodically rebalance back to the index weight. A few of the more popular smart beta strategies are equal-weight, momentum, low volatility, quality, and fundamental index strategies. While they are often grouped together, they are quite different in the manner in which they screen and weight securities, as well as the corresponding results. We view these strategies as a complement to both market-cap and active management.

Our research has shown that many of these strategies have historically delivered excess returns relative to their market-cap equivalents. Certain market environments may reward one strategy versus another. In 2015, momentum was the best performing smart beta strategy as the market was dominated by the FANG stocks (Facebook, Amazon, Netflix, and Google). In 2016, fundamental was the best performing strategy as the markets focused on valuations. We favor fundamental index strategies due to the robustness of the research and the "live" experience of these strategies.

Rick: How do you suggest advisors combine these types of strategies?

Tony: We believe that you need to start by defining the role that each of these strategies plays in a portfolio. We focus on four key levers in building portfolios—*tracking error, loss aversion, alpha, and cost*—and then consider how to weight our strategies across market segments. *Market-cap* strategies have little or no tracking error and are typically the low-cost solution. *Fundamental* strategies have historically delivered alpha across market segments, and are generally more cost effective than active managers. *Active* managers are best equipped to deal with investors' concerns about *loss aversion* as they can play defense. Not all are active managers, but many can deliver better downside protection.

	Domestic Large Cap	Domestic Small Cap	International Large Cap	International Small Cap	Emerging Markets
Market Cap	30%	25%	20%	20%	20%
Fundamental	50%	50%	30%	30%	30%
Active	20%	25%	50%	50%	50%

In the most efficient markets (Domestic Large Cap) [see table], we would allocate 50 percent to fundamental indexing, 30 percent to market-cap, 20 percent to active management. We don't see a lot of persistence in active managers outperforming the passive options. In the least efficient markets (Emerging Markets), we'd allocate 50 percent to active managers, 30 percent to fundamental, and 20 percent to market-cap strategies. Here we believe that there should be some skill in identifying strong companies and avoiding weak ones.

Rick: With the markets' ever-changing nature, how should advisors respond? Should they try to time the market or weather the storm?

Tony: In recent years, there have been a number of events that have caused significant market disruptions: concerns about Greek debt default, Central Bank intervention, Chinese economic slowdown, and Brexit, to name a few. As a result of these dramatic events, investors are demanding insights and advice about how to navigate these challenging waters. Sometimes the best advice is to do nothing, but other times it may be prudent to make subtle shifts in portfolios. We believe in the value of being more tactical in allocating assets. We're not suggesting being all-in or all-out of the markets, but rather making subtle shifts at the margin to help position portfolios. You may want to overweight an undervalued segment of the market or underweight an asset class that has become expensive. You may want to avoid markets with extreme volatility or tactically overweight an interesting investing opportunity.

Being more nimble and flexible may help keep your client engaged in good times and bad. It's also an opportunity to demonstrate your insights and outlook.

Rick: In light of the rapid growth of automated advice (also known as "robo-advice"), your insights show the value of a personal relationship and the ability to react in real time to the ever-changing environment.

Tony: Automated advice shouldn't be viewed as a threat but as an efficient means to scale your business. Firms can either embrace technology, or determine how best to utilize it, or risk becoming obsolete. Technology can help you scale your practice and reach a generation of investors who have become dependent on technology solutions for virtually everything.

It is the combination of technology and personal touch that will resonate with clients. Successful advisors will evolve the way they do business and embrace changes in a positive fashion. While certain things can be automated, personalized advice can never be commoditized. Of course, the balance is how to grow your business while retaining a personal relationship with the client.

Don't Second-Guess the Masters

Successful advisors, leaders with a growth mindset, don't overcomplicate anything. They apply the same basic investment rules to growing their own practice as well as to managing the assets of their clients. A core principle is simply "don't lose," because if you're down 50 percent, you need to be up 100 percent to recoup that 50 percent loss. Said differently, protect the downside because making up big losses becomes very difficult. Tax efficiency makes a difference. Diversify across different asset classes and within asset classes, and dollar-cost average. John Templeton and Warren Buffett, over the course of their careers, have developed a set of simple rules for investment success. Why should we have to make things more complicated than the two greatest investors of all time?

Simple Rules for Investment Success
- Invest for maximum total real return.
- Invest, don't trade or speculate.
- Remain flexible and open-minded about types of investments.
- Diversify. In stocks and bonds, as in much else, there is safety in numbers.

- Listening to market predictions is a waste of time.
- Don't panic.
- Learn from your mistakes.
- Outperforming the market is a difficult task.
- An investor who has all the answers doesn't even understand all the questions.

Wealth management is based on the client's total financial picture. It's not about just managing the investment process; it's following an eight-step process that can help your clients have a better experience and higher probability of achieving their goals:

1. Help your clients understand what comprehensive wealth management is versus just investing. (However, if you don't offer wealth management services, be honest and let the prospect know you only specialize in investment management.)
2. Help them understand why a team is important to achieve their goals.
3. Help them understand the investment process and financial planning process.
4. Help them with estate planning, legacy planning, and so on.
5. Help them manage their debt and cash flow and establish overall good habits on budgeting and saving.
6. Help them with retirement planning needs, life insurance, health and long-term care, and so on.
7. Help them manage the tax liabilities.
8. Help them with succession planning (as needed and appropriate).

The team should have one quarterback—the wealth advisor or financial advisor—along with a planning advisor, a trust advisor, an estate planning lawyer, a tax advisor, an accountant or CPA, and an insurance specialist.

In terms of the advisors managing money, clients want value and the following eight steps provide real value:

1. Help your clients define their short- and long-term goals.
2. Help them fully understand your process and investment philosophy.
3. Help them with asset allocation and diversification across different asset classes.
4. Help them dollar-cost average.
5. Help them rebalance.
6. Help them with behavior coaching, emotional resistance.
7. Help them with tax efficiency.
8. Help them monitor the overall plan and make necessary changes.

"In my nearly 50 years of experience in Wall Street, I've found that I know less and less about what the stock market is going to do but I know more and more about what investors ought to do."

—*Benjamin Graham*

SUMMARY: Part Two

Growing the Business Requires That We Evolve, Lead, and Serve

"Go confidently in the direction of your dreams. Live the life you have imagined."

—*Henry David Thoreau*

Growth mindset is a choice. Growing your wealth management practice is a choice—your choice.

It is up to you to choose your next destination. If you feel you have achieved all your goals and are standing on top of the mountain with your hands up high, find a new mountain. Discover or create a new height to scale. Build something, leave a legacy, be a mentor, make a difference in people's lives, and continue building your business by bringing the next generation into this wonderful business. A leader's greatest motivation is a new challenge. A new challenge may be writing an article or a book. It may be bringing in a new partner.

Recently, I visited Harry, a 77-year-old master wood-worker. Since woodworking is one of my hobbies, I consider Harry my mentor (he is an outstanding teacher). He was working on a bird feeder that was quite elaborate and beautiful, and he was having fun trying to figure out how to get these particular corners the way he envisioned. They were more challenging than he originally thought. Harry doesn't look for the easy-way solution; he looks to challenge himself. Harry derives a great deal of happiness when he tries to solve these challenges. I can see it in his eyes. If you have a growth mindset, new challenges will motivate you.

Creating passion in your life is key. Be open to the possibilities and explore. That's the ultimate growth mind-set. Aristotle was right when he said, "It's the journey, after all, and not the destination." Creating new goals and chal-lenges, whether professional or personal, in order to stay in the zone or flow doesn't just happen. You have to put in the effort. The professional challenge should serve your personal life just as a personal challenge should have an impact on your professional life.

Most of all, don't stop learning and growing, no matter how old you are. If you are climbing to the summit of your first mountain, stay the course and enjoy the journey.

Be a giver, not a taker. Learn from others: everyone has something to teach you. Be a student of the business and always, *always* put the clients' interests first.

The qualities of the most successful advisors in wealth management are, ultimately, very simple:

- Know who you are and whom you want to be.
- Know your business, target market, and model.
- Deliver exceptional service and performance based on client goals.
- Know the true value of a client.
- Know you are the solution the client is buying.
- Aim for optimal performance and know how to get in the zone.
- Know how to move from good to great. Complacency is your enemy. Good is the enemy of great.
- Turn knowledge and information into advice and into growth.
- Be a lifelong learner, ever-growing, ever-evolving.
- Be an effective collaborator and communicator.
- Invest back into the business.
- Don't try to be all things to all people.

For me, the secret of my success is simple. And more importantly it is very clear and has stood the test of time. It isn't some innovative idea, superior talent, or extraordinary discipline. It's a combination of being in the right business, having the right mentors, having some good luck, and most of all being persistent. Giving up was not an option; sports helped me create a belief that perseverance could give me a major advantage. If I look back, not giving up when I got knocked down was my answer. Sports taught me very valuable lessons. And that's what's wonderful about this business. If you're persistent, you can achieve as much success as you can handle for you and your clients.

> "The most important thing in the Olympic Games is not to win but to take part, just as the most important thing in life is not the triumph but the struggle. The essential thing is not to have conquered but to have fought well."
>
> —*Olympic Motto*

PART THREE

What Clients Really Want

High-net-worth clients want it all. Great service, valued advice, performance, and complete transparency. They want white glove treatment at a reasonable price. They want holistic advice that will help them achieve their goals and dreams. Therefore, wealth management is a journey that starts with the destination in mind. The most important part of the journey is figuring out where you want to end up, and how will you get there. It's not exclusively about what your number needs to be. As I said earlier, *wealth management* and *financial investing* are not interchangeable. The more assets, the more complex the planning will be. Therefore, having a professional team on the side of the client is key to maneuvering through this maze. The high-net-worth individuals in the United States are predominately over age 55. Over 90 percent did not inherit their wealth; they are self-made and they worked very hard. In fact, according to *AARP* magazine, 86 percent log more than 50 hours a week. And they also save about 40 percent of their income. They are not mentally and financially ready for retirement, and they dislike salespeople, excessive taxes, and wasting time. What they want more of is time. On average they take six vacations a year, but they are not extravagant, with 77 percent flying economy. They also spend big on kids' education. Good health is important and they spend money on top doctors, good medical insurance, and fresh, high-quality food, as well as a having a commitment to fitness. So, yes, they are very different in some ways but they are also just like everybody else. If you asked them how they became wealthy, they would tell you, hard work, education, smart investing, frugality, and taking risks. We have faced many tumultuous times in the past and I'm sure we will face more in the future. Therefore, the better an advisor can understand the client on the deepest level, the better chance the client will achieve his or her objectives. Helping clients determine whether they need $1 million or $10 million to live a comfortable retirement is a very small part of wealth management. New technologies can calculate the figures pretty quickly—they don't need a human being for those calculations. Additionally, new technology will transform retirement because new devices allow for remote work opportunities and staying connected to family and friends. Because people will live longer they will spend more years in retirement. Technology will give retirees more options and more possibilities.

However, helping them come up with the right life plan by starting with a deep discovery process gets you on the right path. One of the greatest human needs is to be understood. Because we operate in such a fast-paced environment, it takes a mature advisor to ask the most compelling questions. Therefore, clients want wisdom, perspective, and valued advice, not just more information. This means you first have to find out what the client really values from your relationship, since it's not a one-size-fits-all business. Your clients may not even know what they value so you may need to help them identify what's really important to them. And once you know what they value, you need to execute. If you can't deliver value, it's the wrong fit and you should move on. In general, clients want peace of mind, something that means different things to different people. And depending on how old your client is, the following will have varying degrees of importance.

As advisors you have the responsibility and power to impact people's lives. You are the life coach. Investment asset allocation is only a piece of a much bigger puzzle. Research tells us that clients want solid investment returns based on their risk tolerance, great service, and full transparency when it comes to fees, risk, and conflicts. In short, they want trusted advice. New regulations will demand more transparency. Helping people plan and retire successfully starting in their thirties or forties and knowing when it's "enough" is all part of a holistic consultative process. As Winston Churchill said, "The farther back you can look, the farther forward you are likely to see." I have learned that only a small percentage of people retire on their own terms. And the ones that do that I have met over the years had a plan, had some good luck, and had a destination for the next chapter of their life. Clients, too, need to have a growth mindset. Therefore at the end the client wants unabashed client advocacy and stewardship. They want leading edge wealth management solutions that will exceed clients' expectations every day.

Chapter 22

What's Your Number?

"Nature does not hurry, yet everything is accomplished."
—*Lao Tzu*

Everyone has a number and that number for many people, including the advisor, can control one's ability to live a balanced life. In this case, I'm referring to your client's number. What's your number? Wall Street spends hundreds of millions of dollars helping clients answer that question. Fintech firms with retirement-planning software can produce a document informing clients how much money they will need for retirement or what their shortfall may be. All these financial tools are terrific, except these plans are stagnant, and life is anything but. Life happens and circumstances change. The right plan needs to be developed with the advisor navigating the journey and with the client's complete collaboration.

The best way to answer the question, "What's your number?," is to look back at some of the great thinkers like

Plato, Aristotle, and Seneca. Some advisors say the first step starts with a financial plan, but that's really the second step in the process. The first step is to follow this simple formula: Be + Do = Have. The first time I heard this was in 1989 when I attended a two-day workshop on growing my business. As a young advisor, everything that came out of Bob Dunwoody's mouth I made sure to write down. Bob's workshop was by far the most impactful workshop in my life. We became friends and he went on to mentor me. So, the first step is to answer the question: Whom do you want to *be*? In other words, what's your vision? Who are you? What's your destination? Once you know the answer to these questions, you can start *doing* the activities that will make you whom you want to *be*. These actions will result in *having* what you want.

What do people need in order to feel that they are wealthy? By far, as the graph shows, most people believe $5 million is necessary in order to truly feel as if they are wealthy.

Starting Point of Wealth Management

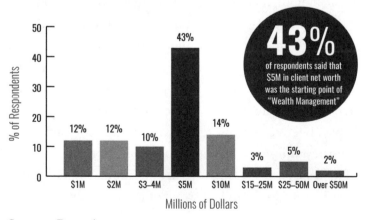

Source: *Barron's*

It makes perfect sense when you think about it. Before people reach their goals they have to create a vision. So, if you're an advisor who wants to double your business, you first have to start with being that $2 million producer now, and follow it up with the actions and tactics of what it takes to be a $2 million producer. Then you will have the success you are seeking. In the case of the client, helping them with the number is helping them understand where they are in terms of their financial goals (Be) and what adjustments they need to make today to move in the directions of their goals (Do) in order to achieve their intended goal (Have). This simple philosophy has been around over 2,300 years. Socrates said, "To do is to *be*"; Plato said, "To be is to *do*"; Descartes said, "I think, therefore I am"; and the Christian Bible states, "As a man thinketh, so shall he be." Each of these great philosophers arrived at the same conclusion. When we think of wealth management, we primarily think about the future, but I suggest looking at the past as well. Ultimately, it's about determining the client's number based on knowing who they are (be). Everything starts with the vision.

Comfortable means something different to every client. That's why the *number* of what you will need is very different from one person to another. People are never all the same. As advisors creating the right balance of communication, the number is very important. Let's say, for example, a client's target retirement number has a $2 million shortfall. Advisors who focus solely on that number create more anxiety for the client. They may offer suggestions to work longer, save more, or get more aggressive in the market. But if we are truly holistic, we have to look at the other side of the balance sheet. Do you really need a house that big? Do you need to live where you're living? Do you need three cars? Do you need the second home? You get the picture. The conversation should not be centered around the actual number; rather it should be about helping your clients discover what's truly important and helping them find meaning and purpose. Helping clients get to the core of what brings them happiness in their lives is what will differentiate you from every other advisor.

A comfortable retirement for some is being able to travel the world on a regular basis. To someone else, it's being able to travel in first class and staying at the finest accommodations. To others, it's being able to do all that with the luxury of their own private plane. For some, it's having a $100,000 cash flow while for others it may be $1 million. As I said, according to *Barron's*, $5 million is where 43 percent of high-net-worth individuals feel rich. For others, $2 million will be just fine, and for others $25 million will not be enough. Many high-net-worth individuals have made a conscious effort to retire. They are staying active much longer and are enjoying the journey.

For most high-net-worth individuals, having a trusted advisor is invaluable. If you are a high-net-worth person and have a trusted advisor, hold onto him or her because she will provide peace of mind. If you're not sure, you may want to look for someone else. As a client, you should never settle when it comes to your future. Look for the right fit for you and your family. Look for someone who can look at your entire financial picture. Your trusted advisor should work with you in a very collaborative way, not dictating what you need. Ultimately, you are the leader and the advisor's job is to inform you, empower you, and help you get to your destination.

High-net-worth clients want:
- Fee transparency
- Good advice (investment performance based on achieving their goals)
- Understanding of concerns and needs (risk)
- Quick and effective resolution of service-related issues

Regardless of what your client's number is, a top advisor will help a high-net-worth individual focus on the four most important areas and deal with the challenges that come with them: market volatility, spending behaviors, taxes and inflation, and longevity.

Market Volatility

Why is it so important to discuss market volatility? People in general are highly emotional about their money. A client's belief system about the market can have a major impact on how she invests and how she reacts to market cycles. Volatility can be heart wrenching; I have seen my share of volatility over the past 34 years. But more importantly, I have seen how clients and advisors react in the middle of the storm. Helping clients deal with volatility does two things: one is to ride out the storm versus jumping out for cover like some people did during the financial crisis of 2007–2009 when the S&P 500 lost approximately 50 percent of its value. The second result in helping clients weather volatility is being appropriately allocated in equities in order for the portfolio to maintain purchasing power. The prolific and highly respected Jeremy Siegel, a professor at the Wharton School of Business, has always been a bull. I've had the opportunity to hear him speak on many occasions, and his enthusiasm about the market and his convictions are very powerful. His famous book, *Stocks for the Long Run*, was first released in 1994, and the fifth edition was released in 2014. In the book, covering a span of more than two centuries, he shows that the total real return of stocks after inflation is 6.7 percent compared to U.S. government bonds' return of 3.6 percent or gold's return of 0.6 percent. Having history as our guide, we have 200 years of volatility and meltdowns, but for the long-term investor, being invested in stocks with a well-diversified portfolio serves them well. The financial collapse that took place in 2008 was more of an aberration than the norm, but history had shown us what can happen when you have irrational exuberance. The Internet has made it easy for individuals, many of whom lack the proper knowledge and expertise, to buy and sell stocks. With a handheld smartphone you can execute a trade in seconds. Investing is a serious and long-term disciplined process. It's not about hunches, entertainment, or gambling. That's why a trusted advisor can make all the difference and provide a customize roadmap for each relationship.

Spending Behaviors

Let's be honest, many of us are materialistic; it's just a matter of to what degree. All we need to do is look in our closets, what percentage of our clothes do we really use? By definition this means being excessively concerned with physical comforts or the acquisition of wealth and material possessions, rather than with spiritual, intellectual, or cultural values. In the past, I saw books only on creating wealth as the key to happiness. Now I'm seeing books, information, and documentaries that focus more on flexibility, thrift, and a life balance and abundance. I hope this means a growing number of the next generation may have more perspective on balance. But, we are still attracted to things we don't need. We all know we own too much stuff. According to the *LA Times*, there are 300,000 items in the average American home. That's hard to believe, but even if it's a quarter of that, it's still a lot. *The Telegraph* reported on a British research study that found that the average 10-year-old owns 238 toys but plays with just 12 daily. Clients always tell us that they want to simplify their lives. They want to be organized and have more free time. Helping them reach a more satisfying state is a definite value add in my book. Because at the end it doesn't matter how much people have accumulated; if they don't have a well-thought-out comprehensive plan that addresses what a reasonable budget is, they will find themselves struggling in retirement. Managing cash flow should be as important as managing a portfolio. A trusted advisor helps them make better decisions. Align your values, mission, and purpose to the net worth you're working with. Excess can clutter our minds, and it can irritate our purpose. Help your clients find the right balance for them.

Generally, the most expensive stage of retirement is the early years, 60 to 70 years old. This makes perfect sense as it's when retirees are most active. A good advisor helps new retirees with their spending. It's about getting inside their heads to understand what's important to them, what brings joy and fulfillment, and what needs to be eliminated from their lives. Helping people connect the dots of what truly brings them satisfaction or helping them discover a new passion could be worth much more than just trying to figure out how to pick up a few more basis points on the portfolio.

Taxes and Inflation

Maintaining purchasing power in a low-interest-rate environment will be key. As life expectancies increase, your clients could easily enjoy 30 or 40 years in retirement and, therefore, those assets need to work for the client and they need to last. After health issues, running out of money is the greatest fear for many. Your clients' portfolios have to be reexamined once they retire. Many are underexposed in equities. Holding onto bonds or other fixed-income investments is a common error because after inflation and taxes they're likely losing money every year. Let the power of compounding work for your clients.

In terms of taxes, take advantage of all the retirement plans available to the client in order to maximize all the benefits. Clients may want to consider moving to a tax-friendly state, selecting alternative investments, or choosing tax-efficient investments and tax-advantage accounts. Estate planning for wealthy individuals is a necessity in order to establish a legal foundation to execute the most effective benefits to their heirs.

Longevity

Average life expectancy in the United States is 78.7 years. A good, long life requires resilience, mental fitness, emotional wellness, physical health, and future planning. Develop and implement an asset protection strategy based on the client's goals and objectives. Utilize insurance in the wealth management process to help mitigate catastrophic losses: life insurance, disability insurance, and long-term care. Develop a business succession plan if the client is an entrepreneur. Security is the cornerstone of wealth management.

This close client–advisor relationship needs to be a consultative process with customized solutions. The questions below should serve as a reminder to both the advisor and the client of a relationship built on trust and transparency.

Every prospective client should ask the advisor the following questions:

- Please tell me about your experience in dealing with a client similar to me.
- Please explain your service model and what can I expect from you and your team.
- How do you charge for the services?
- Can I see a sample financial plan?
- What services do you specialize in?
- What's your investment process and philosophy?
- What makes the client experience unique?
- Are you acting in a fiduciary capacity?
- What questions should I have asked that I didn't ask?

Because a client or prospect will most likely not be reading this book, I would suggest you answer these questions for the client. As a successful and effective advisor, you have to uncover what *wealth* means to your client. Wealth to me is discretionary time and meaningful relationships. It's freedom. Most importantly, it's not a certain number of dollars. I have been servicing and been around high-net-worth clients for three decades and I have learned an awful lot about money, life, success, and accomplishments. These people worked very hard for what they have with countless sacrifices. Unfortunately, too many feel they never have enough wealth. Just like sea water, the more you drink the thirsty or you become.

A confident and competent advisor can help a family deal with their relationship with wealth, help determine what amount of money is enough, and help clients live the life they want and leave a legacy that's significant to them. As Warren Buffett wisely said, "Risk is not knowing what you're doing."

The next generation of investors will have the same ultimate goals of a comfortable retirement, but the way they will connect and communicate with a firm and advisor may be different. After the Great Recession, generations X and Y have become even more cynical and less trusting. They still value their relationship with a trusted advisor, but they require complete transparency and will be more demanding to see value in the relationship.

Retirement means something very different to me than it did for my parents or past generations. And it will mean something different for my children. Bain's Global Wealth Management group profiled 20 companies that make up roughly 10 percent of global assets under management; they augmented that analysis with interviews with more than 100 senior executives in the industry. The analysis confirms a formidable challenge: while clients are more inclined than ever to seek professional wealth management, they are less trusting and more skeptical now.

That puts a premium on building durable, trusting client relationships. A strong client experience creates high levels of customer loyalty, which is vital to increasing profitability. Bain research shows that loyal customers give their financial service providers a larger share of their business, recommend them to friends and colleagues, and cost less to serve.

Therefore helping the client hit the number is not just advising them on investment management; that's only part of the equation. It's helping them make the best life choices about all aspects of their financial life. Helping clients live more fully and with greater peace of mind is not something a robot is likely solve in this century.

Chapter 23

The Good Life

We live in a world of infinite information and constant change. Our clients are seeking peace of mind and they want clarity and perspective from all this noise of information. If you want to help them live the good life and lead them on a path of a more abundant life, you must redefine the client experience. The conversation must go well beyond the investment dialogue. As technology continues to transform financial services and fundamentally changes the relationship clients have with us, it will be that holistic approach that will not become commoditized.

I had the best classroom for the past three decades watching people in pursuit of the good life. As a student of the business, I paid close attention to how clients achieved that success, how they thought about retirement, and choices they made. Since curiosity comes very naturally to me, I would frequently ask—still do—lots of questions. Some advisors would question why I wasn't on topic. And they would be right. I wanted to truly understand why clients made the decision they made. What drives them, what they worry about, why they made certain decisions. Today and for the past 25 years I have been asking and digging deeper about the advisor's mindset. What are advisors most proud of, what were their big mistakes, who are the people that matter most in their lives, and, finally, what drives them to be successful and achieve a life with less anxiety and more purpose? It is from these "off" topics that I learn what's important to people. Because the greatest satisfaction we receive as advisors is when we fulfill our purpose: to make our clients' financial lives better. One of the great fears many of us face is that, despite all our effort and striving, we will discover at the end that we have wasted our life. In *A Guide to the Good Life*, William B. Irvine plumbs the wisdom of Stoic philosophy, one of the most popular and successful schools of thought in ancient Rome, and shows how its insight and advice are still remarkably applicable to modern lives.

It's All about the Journey

Society wants us to believe that we need millions of dollars to have a fulfilling retirement, because we need more of everything—newer, better, faster, bigger. The United States is projected to spend $182 billion in advertising in 2017. That's a lot of ads popping up on your smartphones, iPad, iPhone, TV, and everywhere you look. Helping your clients find balance and stay on the path that gives them more options takes finding that thing or things that provide the fulfillment your clients seek. It may be the next sports car, or maybe not.

What makes a great retirement? For many people it takes three years, sometimes longer, to shed their work identities and fully embrace leisure. Ultimately, it's about one's satisfaction and hunger for joy, community, and purpose. As an advisor, you can give your clients the possibility of a blank canvas and collaborate with them to paint a picture of their future. Everyone's idea of fun is different. The good life requires the willingness to be flexible and to change direction, but most importantly never losing the sense of curiosity.

Having your clients contemplate some of these questions may help you guide them toward their good life:

- Am I learning new things and having new experiences?
- Am I cultivating relationships with people I care about?
- Do I spend time doing the things I enjoy most?
- Am I helping others? Do I feel I am making a contribution to a better world?
- Do I have something to hope for?
- Am I living life with the sense of adventure?

Another way to guide your clients toward the good life is to ask them to complete the following exercise, designed by Laura Nash and Howard Stevenson in their book, *Just Enough*. The exercise helps to determine a client's definition of success, or success profile.

1. On a piece of paper, sketch four intersecting circles. These circles represent the four chambers, or pillars, of success: achievement, happiness, significance, and legacy.
2. Label each circle with one of these words.
3. Then, in each circle write one of the following words: self, family, work, and community.

4. The advisor can help the client discover the client's ideal picture for each of those categories. Mapping success for each of your clients and helping them achieve their goals goes beyond investments. It's about helping your clients define their own personal definition of the good life.

Depending on the age of the client, the pillars of success will change or evolve over time. It will be important to revisit this exercise many times over the course of the advisor–client relationship.

The good life is about following your dreams. It's about focusing on what's important to the client. It's about not letting society influence how you live or dictate what you want. I have always been intrigued and inspired by those people who follow their passion and their dreams regardless of the difficulties or challenges.

I was vacationing in Antigua, one of the Caribbean islands where people are wonderful and the turquoise water makes you feel very relaxed, when my daughter Bianca and I heard a middle-aged couple speaking Italian. I introduced myself and Bianca to them, which sparked a wonderful conversation. Giuliana and Roberto were coming off their 42-foot sailboat, called *Patty Boy*. They had been living at sea for three years. They had crossed the Atlantic Ocean a few months earlier after spending two years in the Greek Islands. At 61 years old, they were living their dream. Roberto had spent 40 years as a limousine driver and Giuliana was a dress designer who worked for herself from home. They both have grown children from previous marriages.

What's amazing is since they lived on a pretty strict budget, when it came time to select a boat they were very careful. The boat they chose was about 10 years old but in excellent condition. They spent several years sailing around their home in Italy so they could get used to the boat and gain experience and confidence before eventually sailing to the Greek Islands, where they spent almost 2 years. Giuliana really enjoyed talking and was a wonderful story-teller. It was simply amazing hearing them speak about the wonderful people they'd met along the way. This passion for living this good life was contagious. They simply lived in the moment, with no crazy schedule and no attachments to material things.

What was the big lesson for me? I can think of several. The most important was that you know when someone is truly wealthy when they have control of their desires and how they spend their time. Therefore, are you time rich or time poor? When I asked Giuliana and Roberto if there was anything they missed or needed or if there was anything that would make their life better, they simply said they didn't need anything. Giuliana and Roberto appreciated every day and were amazed by each beautiful sunrise and sunset. They had a vision, confidence, and mission to sail to the Caribbean. In fact, they never plan to return to Italy. They plan to live on the boat for the next 15 years and eventually settle on a small island and buy a small house by the water. I share this story as a reminder of how two people can show us the possibility of living every day with a sense of curiosity and passion. To break away from materialism, regardless of how much money someone has. People who are trying to win more game have never confronted their demons, and more stuff puts a Band-Aid over these demons. Therefore true wealth is not measured by how big our account is, but how happy we are, and how we enrich others with our gifts.

In the end, living the good life is about living your life by design. The right wealth management team can help the client design this customized plan. And the client's net worth should be measured by their own definition, but you can help them. If we want to live a happy life filled with abundance, we have to make that our choice. Expectations and circumstances will always get in the way, and riding the emotional rollercoaster is part of the journey. If we have reasonably good health, meaningful personal relationships, and the curiosity to keep learning and exploring to make the world a little better, we should be grateful.

> "Be soft, don't let the world make you hard. Be gentle, don't let the people make you difficult. Be kind, don't let the realities of life steal your sweetness and make you heartless."
>
> —*Nurudeen Ushawu*

I've had the privilege to interview a number of outstanding industry leaders for this book and you've seen my conversations with them at various points in the book. One of those interviews was with John Hyland, founder and managing director of Private Advisor Group. John's story is simple, but it is the best example of what it means to have a growth mindset. He reminds us of what's possible. He inspires by deeds not words. We talked a lot about having a vision and its value. But there's more to it than that. John embodies much of what having a growth mindset means. He also walks the walk when it comes to effective recruitment, building the right culture, empowerment, optimism, and, above all, courage.

Rick: Tell me about your story from the beginning, where you started and how you got into the wealth management business.

John: I graduated college in 1989. What I knew from the beginning was two things: I didn't want to be in sales and I didn't want to go into the financial services industry. I didn't know much about what I wanted but those were two things I knew. I probably shouldn't admit all this, but I didn't want those two things because I didn't understand them and I didn't have any sort of comfort level. I didn't like sales, especially sales in that traditional sense. It was a tough job market in 1989, so I started bartending in Morristown, New Jersey, where my father was mayor and freehold director. One Saturday, my father invited me to participate in a charity softball game. I was playing shortstop and a gentleman walked up to me and put his arm on my shoulder and said, "I understand you are Pat Hyland's son and you're looking for a job." This gentleman worked for IDS Financial, which is now Ameriprise, and he asked if I would be interested in being a financial advisor. I said to myself "Wow, I don't really want to be in this world, but this guy captures my attention." He was special. He was my inspiration at that point. Like my father, he taught me through his actions and for me that was the greatest way to learn and it was authentic. Here is a wealthy individual and he would sit down and do cold calling with me on a Saturday morning. How many people would do that? He taught by example.

Rick: So you had a breakout year in 1993. Where did you go from there?

John: I became a district manager at American Express Financial and I was a platinum advisor. I was doing well on the managerial side as well as being an advisor. So I started to head more toward independence, transparency, and objectivity. In 1997, we called LPL as it was the biggest independent brand. That October we moved to LPL in Morristown. We started with four partners and continued on that path.

Rick: What was the vision when you first started?

John: Here's where you get a lot of transparency from me. We decided to set ourselves up as four separate branches. We did this for reasons of future profitability. So you learn by failing, and a couple years later it became apparent that this model wasn't working because we were all duplicating efforts at this point. So Bill Dwyer from LPL called and said we needed to talk because we were horrible at compliance. We were great producers but we weren't good at documentation and recordkeeping. So one of my partners and I immediately went up to Boston. It was on December 10, my birthday. They sat us down and said you either find a different firm or hire a compliance professional to run your compliance model. That was the moment we said, wait a minute, we are doing this all wrong. We had failed. Bill should get all the credit as he changed our trajectory. We immediately hired a compliance manager. Interviewing began the next day and we found a great guy who is still with us today. We all came together as one unit rather than operating as four separate branches. We realized we couldn't do everything. Fast-forward 20 years to today. If it worked this way for the four of us, the model can be an example of creating efficiencies for other advisors. I'd like to tell you our story came from something more inspirational, but it was due to failure that this model came about.

Rick: Very interesting. Failure happens to a lot of people but you happen to be honest about it. When did the vision really start to take off?

John: In 2005–2006, we had an *ah-ha!* moment. That's when the business model started to take shape. Two of the now five partners really saw the vision and we started to invest our time and energy into this model. That was my partner, Pat, and myself. In 2007, Pat and I had a vision and parted ways with the other three partners, buying them out.

Rick: So in 2007, how many advisors worked with you?

John: Twenty for whom we were acting as their Office of Supervisory Jurisdiction (OSJ). We are in a great place today because we saw the opportunity. We kept growing 20 to 25 advisors a year.

Rick: How do you recruit that many people when you are only two people?

John: Pat and I make great partners. Pat is an amazing guy. He has amazing bandwidth and at that time I was more the face of the firm.

Rick: So that's a lot of dinners, lunches, and so on, to try to recruit. That must have been exhausting.

John: I loved it! All of it! I am really into relationships and I have always been. I believe this business has always been about relationships. The ground is shifting as we sit here but it's all going to be about relationships.

Rick: How did you get involved with triathlons?

John: Before I answer that question, let me back up a little. I was on a bad path in the 1990s. I got married in 1994. I was going out every night, drinking a lot, having martinis and steak dinners, and so on. I was a big dude. No exercise, all about fun.

Rick: Why do you feel that's so unusual? Others on Wall Street do that.

John: Well, it wasn't good because it wasn't great balance. Then in 1999, I had an *ah-ha!* moment in my life. It happened in the Giants Stadium parking lot before a game. This will sound crazy, but everyone that day was talking about the Ironman Triathlon because it had been on TV the day before. To me it was an impossible task. The guys I was with were talking about how impossible it was, but also how amazing it was, and I don't know quite how to explain it but something clicked in my head, probably because I love challenges. I am a big fan of deeds, not words, so I didn't talk about it much. So I told myself that day in the parking lot that I am going to do this. I am not going to tell anybody. I went to work the next day, searched the Internet, and found an Ironman Triathlon in Lake Placid in July of the next year. My wife was my biggest supporter.

I bought a bike that week and signed up for swim lessons. Lo and behold I went to Lake Placid in July of 2000 and finished my first Ironman. That was a turning point in my life.

Rick: Obviously, you trained hard. How did your life change? What do you mean by that?

John: Everything gets better when you have balance—relationships, business, health, and so on. So from that point on every year for the next nine years I raced the Ironman. In 2008, I competed in the world championships in Kona, Hawaii. It's absolutely amazing! It became an essential part of my life and I became a better husband, father, and so on. In 2009, I took a year off because I felt I owed it to my wife and kids. I asked myself, "Can I step back?"

Rick: You got sick in 2010. Tell me about that.

John: In April 2010, I get a call from my oncologist. I had joined the Leukemia Society board in 2000 because I had lost an aunt in 1992 to leukemia. So I served on the board as president in 2007/2008 and was involved in fundraising. So I knew a lot about leukemia. My doctor asked if my wife and I could stop by the office that day. I replied that I wasn't coming in and that I wanted to know immediately why he was calling. Clearly with that kind of call you know something's not right. He wouldn't tell me over the phone despite my insistence. Rick, this is still very emotional for me.

Rick: John, I can see this is still very painful.

John: The doctor said you have AML [acute myeloid leukemia]. To you that might not mean a whole lot, but I knew right away what that meant. I asked him right away, am I going to live? There was a long pause and he said there was a lot of work to do. My sister, who is a nurse, and my wife and I went right away to meet with him. I was admitted the next day and immediately started chemotherapy. So with acute leukemia there is an 18 percent survival rate. It was by far the darkest period of my life.

Rick: Fast forward, when did you start seeing hope?

John: About 30 days after I was first admitted to the hospital they got me into remission but I still had 5 more months of chemo ahead of me. While in the hospital, I talked to Pat, my partner, about launching our own RIA. It may seem crazy to some, but I had nothing but time to think and I needed purpose. We came up with a name and got the legal part in order and then we launched PAG in 2011. That's where the tipping point occurred. Now it was about gaining scale. That was the vision. Pat and I are always big on where the puck is going and not where it is. We saw the future and saw the value that we could bring to advisors. We knew it was going to get more complicated from a regulatory standpoint and the trend toward independent wasn't going to stop. Because the advisor has to wear so many hats our value is to remove the daily functions, such as compliance, HR, and so on, so they can better focus on the client. We took all the hats away except for the one they really want to wear, to offer advice. Our value had once been looking at the business through the advisor and had now shifted to looking at it through the eyes of the client.

Rick: You shifted from the advisor experience to the client experience.

John: It's a natural path and evolution. We have a great team and Pat and I give them a lot of autonomy.

Rick: How was your health in 2011?

John: In 2011 I was on the triathlon starting line again and I did a half Ironman. I did it with my wife, Kristin. In 2012, I did the first New York City Ironman. In 2013, I was back in Kona, Hawaii, racing, in the world championships. All of this just 2½ years after being dismissed from the hospital with one of the most deadly forms of cancer.

Rick: So how are you feeling at this point? You must feel everything is behind you and you have a second chance at life.

John: I never look back and ask, "Why me?" I saw it as a blessing. I saw it as one of the greatest things that could have ever happened to me.

Rick: How did cancer change you?

John: I did an Ironman in 2014 and unknowingly I had leukemia again during the race. Two months later I relapsed. I knew while I was racing that something wasn't right. I wasn't performing as well. I had a third relapse in 2016, so that's three times. People survive AML the first time only 20 percent of the time. Rarely does one survive it three times.

Rick: How do you deal with that? It's must be so tough on you and your love ones.

John: It's tough and I am still in the throes of it. They declared me in remission again in August 2016. I still see doctors weekly.

Rick: Did cancer help you see things differently?

John: As I look back on my life, I really wouldn't change anything. I was happy with my life. What did change was perspective came into focus fast, really fast. Things I used to focus on that I thought mattered shifted and I began to focus on what really matters. I started to allocate my time that way. We all say that certain things are important to us but our log of our time is not always in alignment. I have it aligned a whole lot better now. People say "I love my family" and "I love my kids," but now I spend more time with them than ever. I am conscious of the time spent. How I use my time and talent. The market goes down and you lose 20 percent of your portfolio but to me that is not a problem. Any problem that money can solve is not a problem. It's one of my lines. When you get diagnosed with something like cancer, nothing else matters.

Rick: When I lost my mother, my world and perspective changed and I had less tolerance of disingenuous people. My world shrank. How do you deal with relationships now?

John: Yes, it's all about quality versus quantity and how I allocate my time. I am conscious of and understand what's a real problem and what isn't. Not getting upgraded on your flight is not a problem.

Rick: This is an incredibly inspiring story. How do you find balance between health, family, and business?

John: You know the expression, "It's never about the money"? I am being honest when I say it's never been about the money. It's not a factor. It's that DNA inner voice, inner drive, it doesn't go away when you're sick. So continuing to execute on our vision is very important to me. Where I am today is that I have to go on with life as if I am okay. Every once in a while I revisit the idea of retiring but realize there will be a big hole in my life.

Rick: What are some of your final thoughts as you look back at your success? (John was very uncomfortable when I referred to him as successful.)

John: Things have all worked out. I have trouble with success because I am not sure what it really means.

Rick: What's next for you?

John: I am going back to Lake Placid for a half Ironman.

Giving Back

By definition, philanthropy is, whether of a person or an organization, seeking to promote the welfare of others, especially by donating money to good causes and being generous and benevolent. People in all income brackets give lots of money away each year to great causes. In fact, Americans gave an estimated $358.38 billion to charity in 2014, according to the 60th anniversary edition of *Giving USA*. That total slightly exceeded the benchmark year of 2007, when giving hit an estimated inflation-adjusted total of $355.17 billion.

But money plus passing on wisdom and knowledge becomes much more impactful than just writing a check. In a small way, we can all leave a legacy beyond the name on a building or a foundation. Some people I know in their fifties and sixties are finding time to mentor young adults, speak at universities, and work with various charities to provide a specific expertise that's desperately needed. If we are fortunate enough to be in a position to have the luxury to make the world, or even just one person, a bit better, why not fully engage and explore?

We tend to have a passion for something that grabs hold of us early on in our lives. I realized in college that Wall Street was where I needed to be. I wanted to be entrepreneurial, with the opportunity to create wealth and help people with their financial goals. I made one mistake after another: I had the wrong shoes, I lacked confidence, I didn't know how to follow up, I didn't know how to network, I can go on and on. Therefore, mentors have always played a role in my life.

It's no surprise that today I want to play a small part in helping future leaders create the right path to realize their dreams. Investing in our future leaders is good for our economy and humanity. I have created a lecture series for universities to help students connect with industry leaders for advice and strategies to give them a competitive advantage. The feedback has been extremely positive and that's what keeps me going back.

My suggestion is this: if you feel you can help others because you have some specific and special talent, start now. You can improve the circumstances of others.

> "Money is only a tool. It will take you wherever you wish, but it will not replace you as the driver."
>
> —*Ayn Rand*

Conclusion

T he power of your attitude is your choice; a growth
mindset is your choice. Don't allow fear to slow
you down. The Dalai Lama said it best: "Today I
am fortunate to be alive, I have a precious human life, I am
not going to waste it." For many of us on this planet we
have the power to choose happiness over despair, to be the
architects of our own destiny. The truly poor souls are those
who don't have a choice about their circumstances. We are
lucky to be in a business that affords us the opportunity to
help those who are less fortunate. The future of the wealth
management industry will continue to evolve faster than
at any time in past history. The advice business will continue to be a growth business. Our clients are becoming
more sophisticated and therefore will demand a trusted,
competent advisor who will always put their interests first.
Those leaders and advisors who can adapt while also being

brilliant in the fundamentals will win more business and shape how the industry evolves. In the end, those who are successful will be those who *never* stop learning and never lose that curiosity about the world around them. The roadmap is simple, but once again, knowing and doing are miles apart. Start the journey this way:

- Create your vision—define your destination.
- Don't be unconscious in life—too many people are sleepwalking.
- Be aware of your beliefs that may be holding you back.
- Try to live without regrets because at the end nobody cares.
- Understand what you can control and what you can't.
- Live in the world of possibilities, not limitations.
- Always put the client's interests ahead of everyone else's.
- Enjoy the process by getting into the zone.
- Never jeopardize your integrity.
- Choose growth and happiness over fear and anxiety.

> "It is not the critic who counts; not the man who points out how the strong man stumbles, or where the doer of deeds could have done them better. The credit belongs to the man who is actually in the arena, whose face is marred by dust and sweat and blood; who strives valiantly; who errs, who comes short again and again, because there is no effort without error and short-coming; but who does actually strive to do the deeds; who knows great enthusiasms, the great devotions; who spends himself in a worthy cause; who at the best knows in the end the triumph of high achievement and who at the worst, if he fails, at least fails while daring greatly, so

that his place shall never be with those cold and timid souls who neither know victory nor defeat."

—*Theodore Roosevelt*

The very fact that you have engaged in this leadership dialogue shows that you have the desire to improve your game and live with greater purpose. As the wealth management industry continues to experience transformation, these characteristics will serve you well. Technology will continue to change the way our clients interact with us, the choices they have, and the way we do business in fundamental ways. Through this ongoing, never-ending process, the tools we use will change, our roles will change, our services will change, and the regulations that govern us will change. Basically, everything will change except the qualities that define a great leader and the importance of leadership to the success of any organization or advisor.

Leading is not an easy task. It requires strength of character, commitment, and execution of both personal and professional visions. It demands that you show up, fully, every day. It requires a growth mindset.

"The human mind once stretched to a new idea never never regains to its original dimension."

—*Oliver Wendell Holmes*

Suggested Readings

Amen, Daniel G., and Tana Amen. *The Brain Warrior's Way*. Penguin Random House (2015).

Brown, Brené. *Daring Greatly: How the Courage to Be Vulnerable Transforms the Way We Live, Love, Parent and Lead*. Penguin Random House (2012).

Buffett, Warren E. *The Essays of Warren Buffett: Lessons for Corporate America*. The Cunningham Group & Carolina Academic Press (1998).

Carnegie, Dale. *How to Win Friends and Influence People*. Simon and Schuster (1936).

Cohen, Elliot D. *What Would Aristotle Do? Self-Control through the Power of Reason*. Prometheus Books (2003).

Collins, Jim. *Good to Great: Why Some Companies Make the Leap and Others Don't*. Harper Business (2001).

Csikszentmihalyi, Mihaly. *Flow: The Psychology of Optimal Experience*. Harper & Row (1990).

Demartini, John F. *Count Your Blessings: The Healing Power of Gratitude and Love* (2012).

Drucker, Peter. *Managing Oneself* (1999, 2008).

Duhigg, Charles. *The Power of Habit* (2014).

Dweck, Carol S. *Mindset: The New Psychology of Success*. Ballantine Books (2006).

Emmons, Robert A. *Thanks! How the New Science of Gratitude Can Make You Happier* (2007).

Emmons, Robert A., and Michael E. McCullough. *The Psychology of Gratitude* (2004).

Ferguson, Niall. *The Ascent of Money: A Financial History of the World.* Penguin Press (2008).

Frankl, Viktor. *Man's Search for Meaning.* Becon Press (1946).

Gardner, Howard. *Creating Minds: An Anatomy of Creativity Seen through the Lives of Freud, Einstein, Picasso, Stravinsky, Eliot, Graham, and Gandhi.* Basic Books (1993).

Gardner, Howard. *Changing Minds: The Art and Science of Changing.* Harvard Business Review Press (2004).

Goleman, Daniel, Richard Boyatzis, and Annie McKee. *Primal Leadership: Learning to Lead with Emotional Intelligence.* Harvard Business Press (2002).

Grano, Joseph J., with Mark Levine. *You Can't Predict a Hero: From War to Wall Street, Leading in Times of Crisis.* Jossey-Bass (2009).

Grant, Adam. *Give and Take: A Revolutionary Approach to Success.* Viking (2013).

Harvard Business Review and Daniel Goleman. HBR's 10 Must-Reads on Emotional Intelligence (2015).

Koch, Charles G. *Good Profit: How Creating Value for Others Built One of the World's Most Successful Companies.* Crown Business (2015).

Kouzes, James M., and Barry Z. Posner. *Credibility: How Leaders Gain It and Lose It, Why People Demand It* (2011).

_____. *Finding the Courage to Lead* (2013).

_____. *The Leadership Challenge: How to Make Extraordinary Things Happen in Organizations* (2012).

Lesowitz, N., and M. B. Sammons. *Living Life as a Thank You: The Transformative Power of Daily Gratitude* (2009).

Michelli, Joseph A. *The New Gold Standard: Five Leadership Principles for Creating a Legendary Customer Experience Courtesy of the Ritz-Carlton Hotel Company.* McGraw-Hill Education (2008).

Morrell, Margot, and Stephanie Capparell. *Shackleton's Way: Leadership Lessons from the Great Antarctic Explorer.* Penguin Books (2002).

Morris, Tom. *If Aristotle Ran General Motors: The New Soul of Business.* Holt (1998).

Nash, Laura, and Howard Stevenson. *Just Enough: Tools for Creating Success in Your Work and Life.* Wiley (2004).

Oechsli, Matt. *Elite Financial Teams: The 17% Solution.* Wealth Management Press (2009).

Pack, M. Scott. *The Road Less Traveled: A New Psychology of Love, Traditional Values and Spiritual Growth*. Touchstone (1988).

Peters, Tom, and Bob Waterman. *In Search of Excellence* (1982).

Pirsig, Robert M. *Zen and the Art of Motorcycle Maintenance* (1974).

Rather, Tom. *StrengthsFinder 2.0* (2007).

Schroeder, Alice. *The Snowball: Warren Buffett and The Business of Life* (2009).

Sheehy, Gail. *New Passages: Mapping Your Life across Time*. Random House (1995).

Stanfield, R. Brian. *The Courage to Lead, Transform Self, Transform Society*, Second Edition (2012).

About the Author

Rick Capozzi is a highly regarded industry leader in financial services, with a 34-year track record of success in senior leadership positions with the world's largest organizations, including Merrill Lynch, Wells Fargo, Morgan Stanley, and UBS. As national sales manager at Morgan Stanley, Rick was responsible for sales and asset growth. Rick was a successful branch manager at UBS winning many national awards and went on to become regional president at Wells and regional director at Morgan Stanley. Rick led both regions from nearly last to first position in the country by applying his sound principles, proven strategies, and actionable tactics.

Rick is currently president of Capozzi Advisory Group, LLC, a global consulting and training firm. He delivers hundreds of keynotes a year to financial services organizations. He opens his playbook to bring real-world experience and deep industry knowledge to advisors and managers, offering proven strategies and solutions to help them achieve personal and business growth. His workshops and keynotes on leadership and wealth management strategies for high-net-worth clients have helped tens of thousands of financial professionals around the world become more successful in growing their business. Rick has created and delivered over a thousand keynotes to many of the top wealth management organizations in the world, in Asia, Middle East, Europe, and North America.

rick@capozziadvisorygroup.com

tel: (201)-891–9405

LinkedIn: https://www.linkedin.com/in/rickcapozzi/

Capozzi Advisory Group

- Capozzi Advisory Group delivers presentations and keynotes on game-changing strategies to grow a wealth management business. Each presentation is customized based on the client's objectives. Rick has created and delivered keynotes or workshops around the world. The following is a small sample of the organizations; **U.S. Trust, Northern Trust, Morgan Stanley, UBS, Merrill Lynch, Wells Fargo, PIMCO, PNC, SunTrust, LPL, HighTower Advisors, Focus Financial Partners, Banca Mediolanum, TD Bank, KeyBank, BB&T, Citigroup, Fifth Third Bancorp, Bank of Oklahoma, CIBC Atlantic Trust.**

For more information, please visit CapozziAdvisoryGroup.com.

Index